1

4

7

10

2

5

8

11

3

6

9

12

D1372615

13

16

19

22

14

17

20

23

15

18

21

24

25

28

32

35

26

29

33

36

27

30

34

37

31

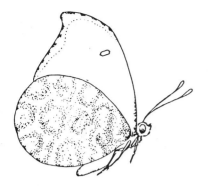

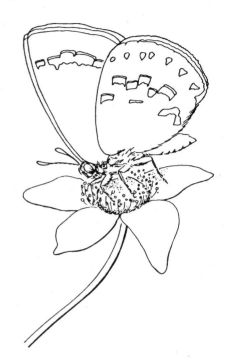

A Field Guide
to Butterflies
Coloring Book

Roger Tory Peterson
and Robert Michael Pyle

Illustrated by Sarah Anne Hughes

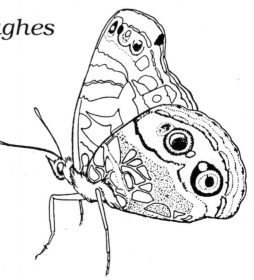

Sponsored by
the National Wildlife Federation
and the National Audubon Society

Houghton Mifflin Company   Boston

Introduction

Watching butterflies is a visual activity; like birdwatching or "birding," it trains the eye. But we can usually approach butterflies more closely than we can birds. We do not need binoculars to see them well.

Most of you who are fascinated by butterflies, if you live in the eastern or central parts of the United States or Canada, will want to own *A Field Guide to the Butterflies.* Or, if you live in the West, its soon-to-be-published counterpart, *A Field Guide to Western Butterflies.* These guides offer shortcuts in recognizing even the most confusing butterflies, using little arrows that point to the special features or marks by which one kind of butterfly may be known from another. Some, like the Monarch, are readily distinguished from all other butterflies except for one — its mimic, the Viceroy. In the *Field Guide* an arrow points to the black line across the lower wing, a line that the Monarch lacks.

Even a person who is colorblind can become skilled at identifying most butterflies by the shape of the wing, the pattern, venation, and even the manner of flight; but, for most of us, color is the first step. This coloring book will sharpen your observations and condition your memory for the days you spend outdoors. By filling in the colors during evenings at home, or on winter days before the Mourning Cloaks make their appearance on the first warm day of early spring, you will be better informed about the various butterflies that will emerge as the season advances.

Many groups of butterflies are basically similar in color. Sulphurs are usually yellow, fritillaries orange, blues blue, wood nymphs brown. Basic color is a useful first clue when putting names to them, but color alone is not enough to identify most butterflies on the species level. Most sulphurs, for example, are yellow. You must also look at other details to narrow your butterfly down to a Common Sulphur, a Dogface, an Orange Sulphur, or whatever. Nevertheless, color is step number one.

There are literally hundreds of species of butterflies in North America. In this coloring book we can show only a selection. Some of the most familiar butterflies are those that feed on the nectar offered by the common roadside flowers, many of which are shown in *A Field Guide to Wildflowers Coloring Book.*

A coloring book such as this will help your color perception, but will not teach you to draw unless you copy the basic line drawings, so artfully prepared by Sarah Anne Hughes. You might even try to sketch the butterflies you see, if only roughly in pencil. Most of you may find colored pencils best suited for coloring this book, but if you are handy with brushes and paints, you may prefer to fill in the outlines with watercolors. Crayons, too, can be used. But don't labor; have fun. That is what this coloring book is all about.

Roger Tory Peterson

About This Book

Butterflies mean color, lively flight, the freshness of spring, and the freedom of summer. But how many people really take time to look at butterflies? Most of us chase butterflies as children, then forget about them as we grow older. This is a pity, for these bright insects offer much to enrich our lives. Coloring butterflies may be a way for you to get to know them in the first place, or to get back to butterflies if you have forgotten how delightful they can be.

For a generation, Professor Alexander B. Klots's *A Field Guide to the Butterflies of North America, East of the Great Plains* has been a passport to pleasure through butterflies. (Soon this book will be revised, and joined by a companion Peterson Series volume for western butterflies.) But if going straight from the bush to a book is like a plunge into cold water for you, this coloring book may provide a gentler introduction to butterfly identification. It is intended for all persons, of all ages, who love butterflies. From here, you may wish to go on to more detailed books.

How to Use This Book

Butterflies are more difficult to get close to than flowers are, but easier than birds. Their markings are quite distinctive, their patterns often complicated. By getting to recognize these features through this book, you will find it simpler to learn them in the field.

Lycaenid Egg

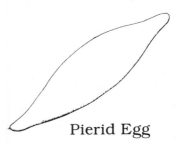

Pierid Egg

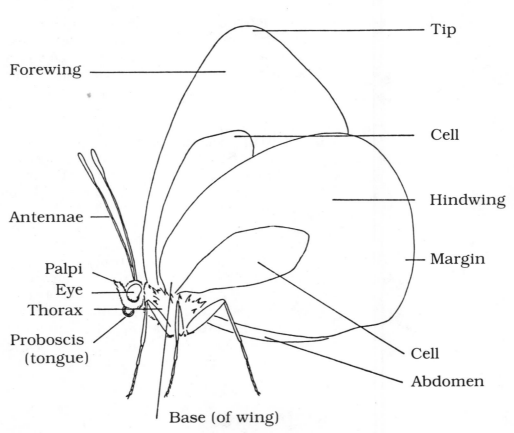

Tip

Forewing

Cell

Hindwing

Antennae

Margin

Palpi

Eye

Thorax

Proboscis
(tongue)

Cell

Abdomen

Base (of wing)

Spicebush
Swallowtail
Larva

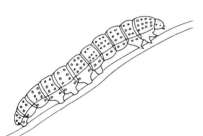

Cloudless Sulphur
Larva

Parts of a Butterfly. The simple diagram on p. 4 shows the makeup of a typical butterfly. You need to become familiar with its parts for identification. Every butterfly has four wings, each with an upperside (above) and an underside (below). The wings may be held in an open or closed position, depending upon what a butterfly is doing — basking in the sun, hiding from predators, or courting, for example. The colors on the wings come from scales. These are tiny shingles that cover both butterflies and moths, setting them apart from all other insects. Some of these scales are colored by pigments, others are shaped so they bend the light like a prism to create iridescent or metallic colors. Because scales fall off or fade as a butterfly ages, its colors may change somewhat. The patterns on the wings serve many functions — camouflage (such as false eyespots to fool predators), attracting mates, and so on. These patterns may vary from place to place and often differ between sexes.

In the descriptions, I refer to the upper- and undersides of the wings; to the base, cell, tip, and margins or borders of wings, and to forewings and hindwings. All these are labeled on the diagram. The wings and legs attach to the thorax, the middle of the body between the head and the abdomen. On the head are the large, many-faceted eyes, the knobbed antennae (moths have pointed ones), and the coiled, drinking-straw tongue or proboscis. Usually the body parts are brown or black, but they may be covered with colorful, furry scales.

Life History. Butterflies have four life stages. The adults mate and the female lays eggs, which hatch into tiny caterpillars or larvae. These, feeding on particular kinds of host plants, grow and shed their skins. Finally, out comes the chrysalis or pupa. Within this case, one of the greatest miracles in nature takes place as the larval material rearranges itself to become the adult butterfly. When it is ready, the butterfly emerges, spreads and dries its wings, and begins the cycle once more.

There is not enough room to show the life-history stages of every butterfly pictured in this book, but a few typical examples appear on these pages. They are as distinctive and interesting as the butterflies themselves. Watch for them on your field trips — it is very exciting to rear a butterfly from the egg, caterpillar, or chrysalis, and to watch the amazing changes take place before your eyes.

Identification. Just like birds, most butterflies possess field marks — special features that will help you in telling them apart. The Peterson system of locating those field marks and using them to identify species works very well with butterflies. The drawings in this book emphasize the field marks. By coloring them in, you will learn them more quickly. Other facts — such as locality, plant association, and flight period — help in identification as well. Keep a field notebook and write down your observations faithfully. Describe what you see and draw pictures.

Spotting Butterflies. First you must find butterflies. The most important factor is sunshine. While some butterflies come out on cloudy days, most are sun worshippers. Different species fly at different times, from early spring to late autumn, and a few even fly in midwinter as long as the days are sunny and warm. Butterflies seek flowers, so you must do the same. Not all gardens and wildflowers have nectar that is equally attractive to butterflies, so you will want to learn which flowers in your area are their favorites. Phlox, thistle, milkweed, butterfly bush, and dandelions are always good. Butterflies also love tree sap, rotting fruit, carrion, and animal scat. Damp patches of sand or mud attract butterflies — swallowtails, sulphurs, blues, and skippers are avid mud-puddlers. When you can identify the plant on which the butterfly's caterpillar feeds, you have another good clue for finding it. The habitat scenes in this book show some good kinds of places for hunting butterflies. You will be sure to find others.

Having once located butterflies, you then need to approach them ever so gently. Move slowly and make no quick movements. This way you can creep very close — close enough to take a butterfly onto your finger or to observe it with a hand lens. Binoculars are useful for spotting butterflies that are too high, far, or wary to approach.

Butterfly Diversity. The word *diversity* refers to how many different kinds there are. In North America, butterflies are about as diverse as birds, much less so than flowers. Since we can picture only a sampling, we have selected some you will recognize as old friends, some you will want to become acquainted with in your area, and some that will encourage you to visit exciting new butterfly habitats. Most of those included are common species. Others are especially beautiful or interesting for their natural history. Their colors and patterns range from brilliant and striking to soft and simple. Taken together, they should give you a sense of the diversity of butterflies.

Scientists don't all agree on how many butterfly families there are. Within the brush-footed family I have included several groups that others consider to be separate families. Regardless of family names, you will quickly see how all longwings fit together but differ from fritillaries, for example. It is more important to get to know the butterfly itself as a living creature than to worry about classification. With common sense and open eyes, you will gain a feel for evolutionary relationships among butterflies. Observing them and coloring their pictures are useful ways of getting started.

6

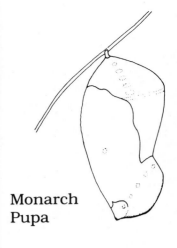

Monarch
Pupa

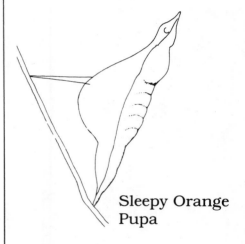

Sleepy Orange
Pupa

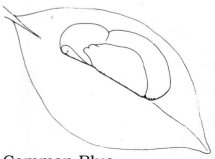

Common Blue
Pupa

Butterfly Conservation and Enjoyment

Many butterflies can live only in certain places, as the habitat scenes show. If those places are destroyed, the butterflies die out. We have included several endangered species that prove this point — Schaus' Swallowtail, Atala, Mitchell's Marsh Satyr, and the Dakota Skipper. Rarities like these should be collected sparingly, if at all. But for the most part, it is habitat destruction rather than collecting that threatens rare butterflies. If you go on to study insects in depth, you will probably form a collection. With care and common sense, insect collecting need not be damaging and it is necessary for the progress of entomology (the scientific study of insects). But most butterfly lovers would prefer to enjoy butterflies alive. They do so by watching, photographing, or gardening for butterflies. This coloring book gives you another kind of butterfly "collecting" that leaves the butterfly in the field or forest. Remember to help conserve wildlife habitats, so that butterflies will survive for their sake and for ours.

I learned about butterflies along a homely Colorado canal. Since then I have studied them in the high Rockies, the jungles of New Guinea, and the deserts of Central Asia. It is thrilling to chase butterflies around the world, but the excitement has never eclipsed the pleasure of boyhood butterfly hunts along that prairie ditch. I'm sure there is such a place near your home — a meadow, a marsh, a wood, or a park — where you can find native butterflies. Wherever you find them, colorful butterflies will give you a fresh look at life.

Robert Michael Pyle

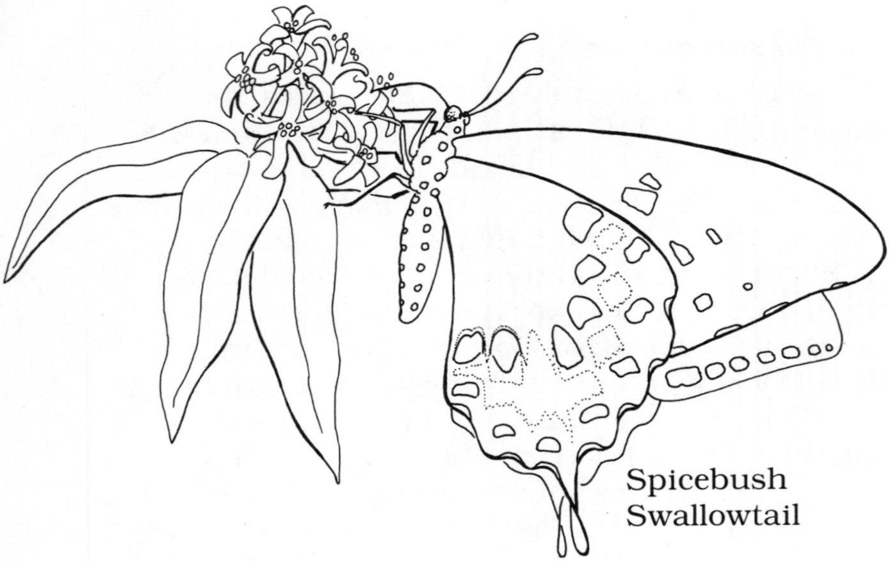

Swallowtails

The largest and some of the most colorful butterflies belong to the family Papilionidae, which includes the swallowtails. Most swallowtails have tails on their hindwings that serve to distract birds from the butterfly's body. The family also includes the very different-looking, waxy white and red-spotted parnassians, which live in northern mountains. Swallowtails are found in almost every part of the world.

Spicebush Swallowtail Eastern in its range, the Spicebush takes its name from its caterpillar's host plant. Often found in fields and gardens, especially near woods. Here it is nectaring on bush honeysuckle. The velvety black wings and body are yellow-spotted. Two rows of bright orange spots enclose starry clouds of blue or green scales on the hindwings. (1)

Pipevine Swallowtail Small greenish spots run around the edges of the wings. The forewings are jet black, but the hindwings with their tails shimmer with a brilliant blue or blue-green iridescence. The caterpillars feed on poisonous pipevines, which give the adults a bad taste. Birds avoid them and several other butterflies that have come to mimic the Pipevine. Shown here on Japanese honeysuckle. (2)

Tiger Swallowtail Common in every eastern city, this big, bright swallowtail loves to visit phlox and thistle for nectar. A similar species lives throughout the West. Both are lemon-yellow with black tiger-stripes. The underside, as shown here, has a field of blue patches along the outer part. Orange spots run along the outer edge of the hindwing. Here it is visiting garden phlox. Shown in Butterfly Garden as well (p. 64). (3)

Spicebush
Swallowtail

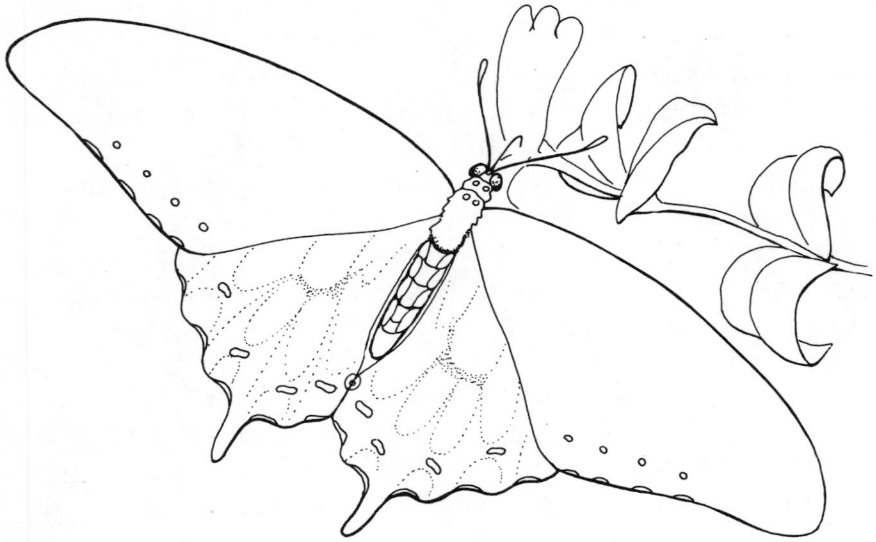

Pipevine
Swallowtail

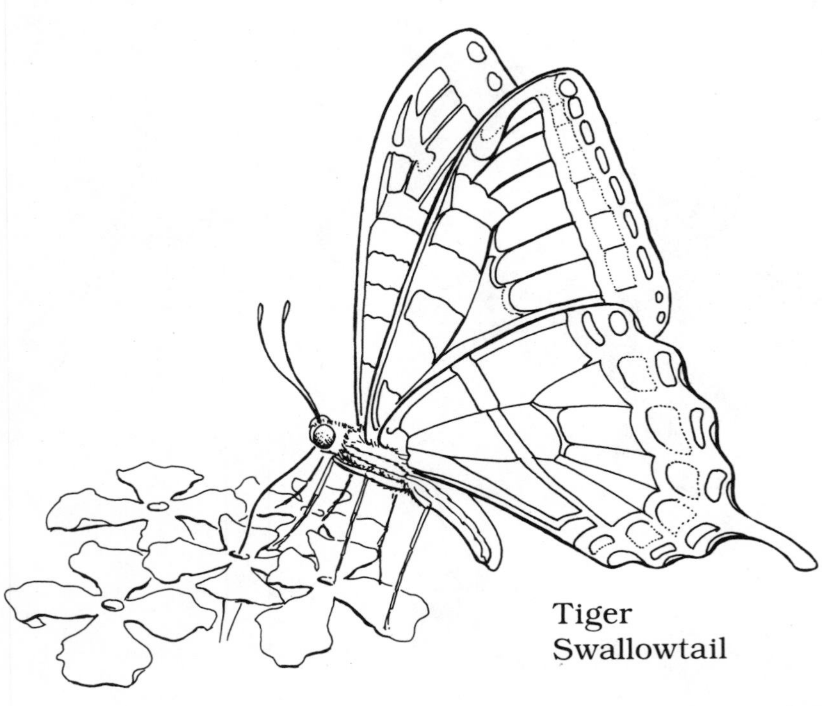

Tiger
Swallowtail

Palamedes Swallowtail Also pictured in the scene of the Southeastern Woods (p. 41), where it can be abundant. Palamedes has very broad wings, making it a fine flier. The lower surface is basically dark brown, with yellow spots. A row of orange chevrons crosses the hindwing, each lined with brilliant blue. Orange-red spots edge the wing to below the long, rounded tail. (4)

Giant Swallowtail This is the largest butterfly in North America, reaching nearly 6 inches across. The big, saddled caterpillar, known as the Orange Dog, feeds on citrus. It resembles a bird dropping, so predators often leave it alone. The wings are mostly black with yellow bands above, yellow with black bands below. Both sides have an orange spot near the tip of the body, with blue crescents. Here two Giants nectar on lilac. (5)

Zebra Swallowtail The most swallowtailed of all our swallowtails. Black stripes alternate with creamy white bands, and a scarlet streak crosses the middle of the hindwing. A pair of red spots, then two blue ones, lead down to the long tail. You will find this striking butterfly only where pawpaw grows, for the larva feeds on it. (6)

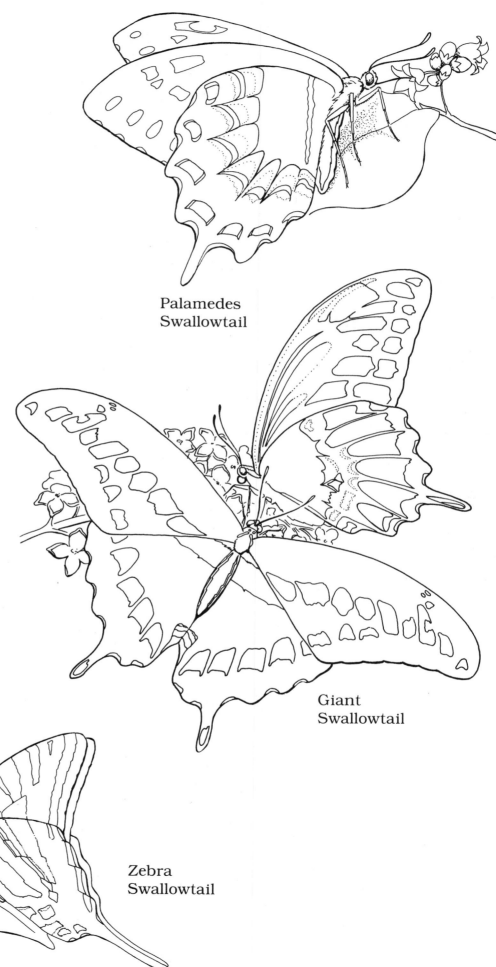

Palamedes
Swallowtail

Giant
Swallowtail

Zebra
Swallowtail

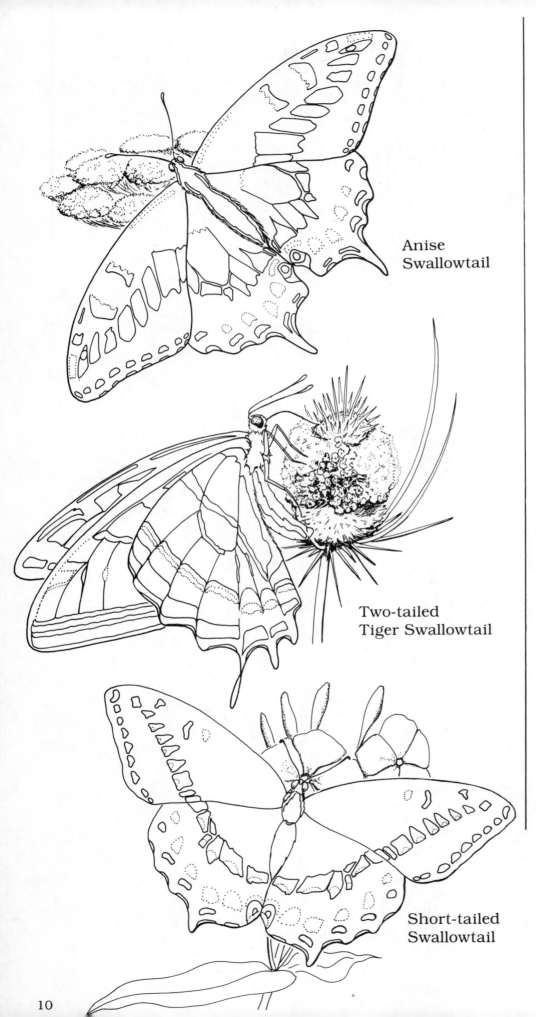

Anise
Swallowtail

Two-tailed
Tiger Swallowtail

Short-tailed
Swallowtail

Anise Swallowtail The Anise and its relatives differ from the Tigers by having yellow bands across black wings instead of black stripes on yellow. Blue spots rim the hindwings, leading down to the black-pupilled orange spot inward from the black tails. Anise Swallowtails commonly seek their mates on mountaintops. (7)

Two-tailed Tiger Swallowtail So-called because it sports a pair of tails on each hindwing. The bright yellow wings and abdomen carry narrow black stripes. A field of blue lies inside the marginal yellow spots, and the two spots below the tails are red-orange. Two-tailed Tigers soar through western canyons where wild cherries provide nectar and host-plant forage. This one is visiting teasel. (8)

Short-tailed Swallowtail Only in the Maritime region of Canada can this lovely swallowtail be found. Like other black swallowtails, its larval host plants are in the carrot family. Color it very black, with yellow spots, give each spot an orange flush toward the outer edge, and add blue between the yellow spot rows of the hindwing. (9)

Eastern Black Swallowtail It is pictured in the Eastern Swamp Scene on p. 13. This is a common swallowtail in gardens, meadows, and wetlands east of the Rockies. Bright orange spots parallel the yellow spots below, with clouds of blue scales between them. Only the corner spot near the body is orange above. Look for it in your garden around the carrots. (10)

Schaus' Swallowtail Also known as the Ponceanus Swallowtail, it is a federally designated Endangered Species. Destruction of its tropical hardwood hammock habitat in Florida has brought it near extinction, but efforts are under way to save it. The general color below is mustard yellow with brown bands. The big patch on the hindwing is rusty-red, lined by sky-blue on its outer edge. Shown here on red hibiscus, a favorite flower of many swallowtails. (11)

Old World Swallowtail Mostly an arctic butterfly in North America, it is more common in Europe and Asia. The black wings have broad yellow bands and are peppered with yellow scales near the body. A row of blue-scaled patches runs around the hindwing above the black tails, ending in a large orange spot that is rimmed with black and capped with blue. (12)

Oregon Swallowtail A denizen of the hot basalt canyons of the Columbia River country, this beauty is the official Oregon State Insect. It has the same pattern as the Anise and Old World Swallowtails, but its bands and spots are deeper yellow. The orange spot with a blue cap on the hindwing has a flattened black dot in it; the dot is round on the Anise and missing in the Old World. (13)

Phoebus Parnassian Appears in the Alpine Scene, p. 20. Although the parnassians scarcely resemble swallowtails, they are in fact quite closely related. Phoebus is waxy white in color, with charcoal edges to the forewing, black spots near the base, and two or three ruby spots in between. Each hindwing, inwardly edged with black, bears a bright red spot near the middle. (14)

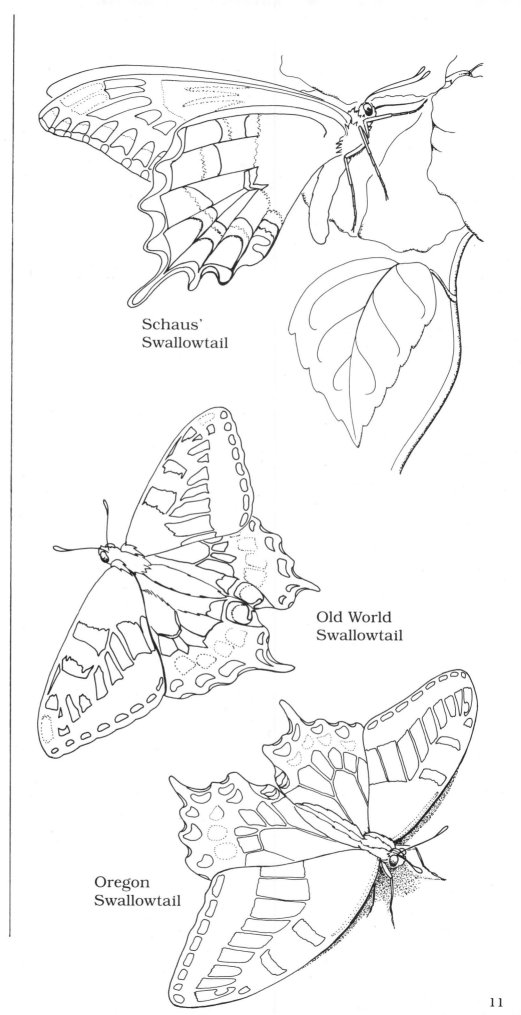

Schaus'
Swallowtail

Old World
Swallowtail

Oregon
Swallowtail

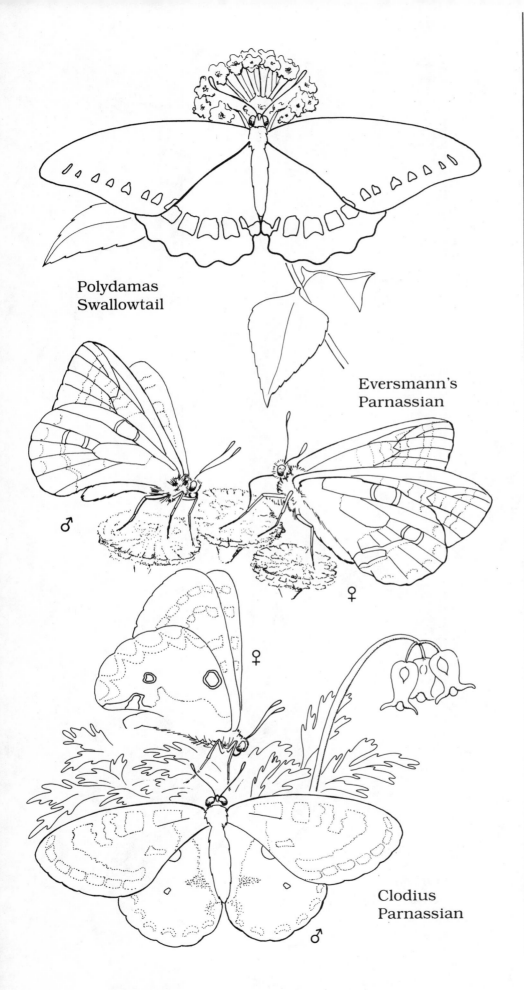

Polydamas Swallowtail

Eversmann's Parnassian

Clodius Parnassian

Polydamas Swallowtail Also called the Gold Rim because its black-velvet wings are neatly margined with yellow spots above. The underside shows red spots on wings and body. These are thought to warn birds away, since the Polydamas acquires the bad taste of pipevines, its caterpillars' host plants. Nectaring on lantana. (15)

Eversmann's Parnassian Alaska and Northwestern Canada are the only places in the New World where this parnassian is found. It is the only yellow parnassian. The male is brighter yellow with two red spots on each wing below, while the female is paler and has its red spots running together into a streak on the underside of the hindwing. (16)

Clodius Parnassian Parnassians are western butterflies. Clodius flies lower in the mountains than Phoebus and differs by lacking any red spots on the forewing, scarlet appearing only in the central spots of the hindwings. Otherwise it is milky white with black spots. Females are dusky and largely transparent, and have more red spots underneath. Caterpillars eat bleeding hearts. (17)

Eastern Swamp Scene (p. 13)

The Eastern Swamp is a wet world, steamy and buggy on a summer's day. Here the female Eastern Black Swallowtail (10) flirts with Queen Anne's lace, either to sip nectar or to lay an egg. The Bronze Copper (64) basks on sedges, as a Swamp Metalmark (91) flies past. Nectaring on the blue vervain is the Silver-bordered Fritillary (111). Now that most of the bogs it prefers have been drained, Mitchell's Marsh Satyr (168) takes refuge here.

Eastern Swamp Scene

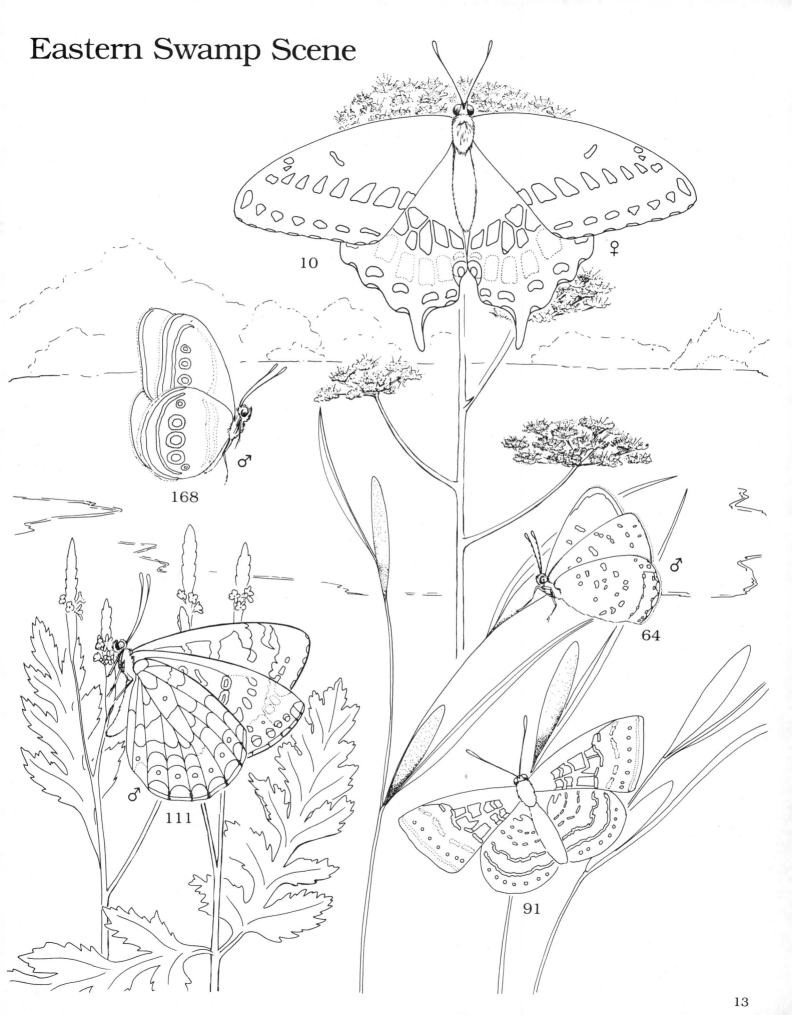

10

168

64

111

91

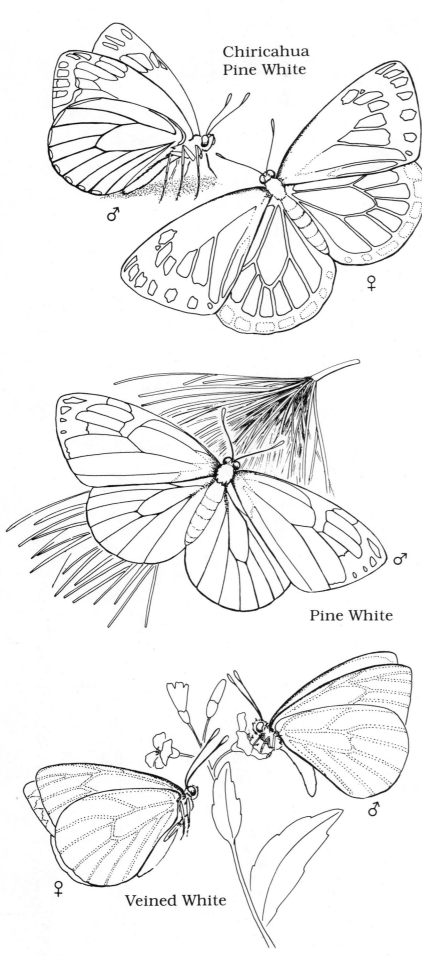

Chiricahua
Pine White

♂

♀

Pine White

♂

Veined White

♀

Whites and Sulphurs

The family Pieridae includes many common and familiar butterflies of town and country. Sulphurs tend to live on pea family plants, while most of the whites have mustard family host plants. Several pierids migrate in huge numbers, often out to sea. While some are farm and garden pests, whites and sulphurs add a great deal of color to the world. The marblewings and orange-tips, also in the family, are among our prettiest butterflies.

Chiricahua Pine White An autumn flier in the Chiricahua Mountains of Arizona, this white occurs around the ponderosa pines its larvae feed on. The males and females are dramatically different looking. The underside of the male, shown here, is white with black veins and a large black forewing patch. The female is halloween-colored — bright reddish orange with black veins, wing margins, and forewing cells. (18)

Pine White Another browser on pine needles, found throughout much of the West. Its upper side is all chalky white except for an intricate pattern of black around the outer part of the forewing. The underside of the females' hindwings is wreathed in red. In some years this butterfly erupts into vast flights of millions of individuals. (19)

Veined White The Veined White occurs in much of the Northern Hemisphere. Individuals can vary greatly in appearance. This is a typical spring Veined White with heavily marked veins below. The veins appear olive-gray against a white background. Also called Mustard White after the family of its chosen host plants. One of these is cardamine, on which it is nectaring here. (20)

Falcate Orangetip   So-called because of the hooked wing tip, which is surrounded by orange in the male. Otherwise white above with a black spot in the forewing cell. The female is shown here with her underside in view. She is delicately but beautifully marbled with yellowish green scales. Seek it in spring in the East around cresses, mustards, and nectar flowers like this spring beauty. (21)

Great Southern White   This big butterfly of the Southeast is mostly white, with black triangles pointed in along the forewing margins. A very dark form of the females occurs, most commonly in summer. Normally fairly numerous, the Great Southern White sometimes builds up into huge masses of butterflies, which then emigrate in search of fresh food. (22)

Cabbage White   Every garden with members of the cabbage family has these hardy whites fluttering about it in summer. A European species, it was introduced over one hundred years ago to North America. Since then it has spread to nearly every part of the land. Mostly a pure, creamy white, it has black spots on the forewings, charcoal forewing tips, and a yellow underside hue. (23)

Sara Orangetip   When you see this butterfly in flight, it looks like two little orange flags fluttering on the breeze. Then you notice the white part connecting them. A delicate spring butterfly of the West, it lives from the sea to the high mountains. The male has milky white wings with brilliant orange tips bordered with black. He sips nectar from wild strawberry. The female has pale yellow wings, also with orange tips, and the underside of her hindwings is delicately marbled with grass-green scales. (24)

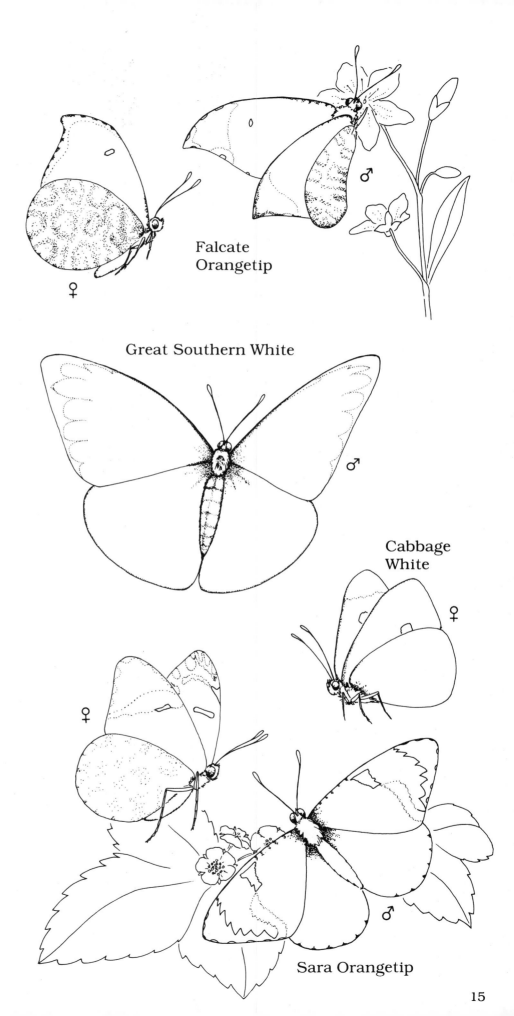

Falcate
Orangetip

Great Southern White

Cabbage
White

Sara Orangetip

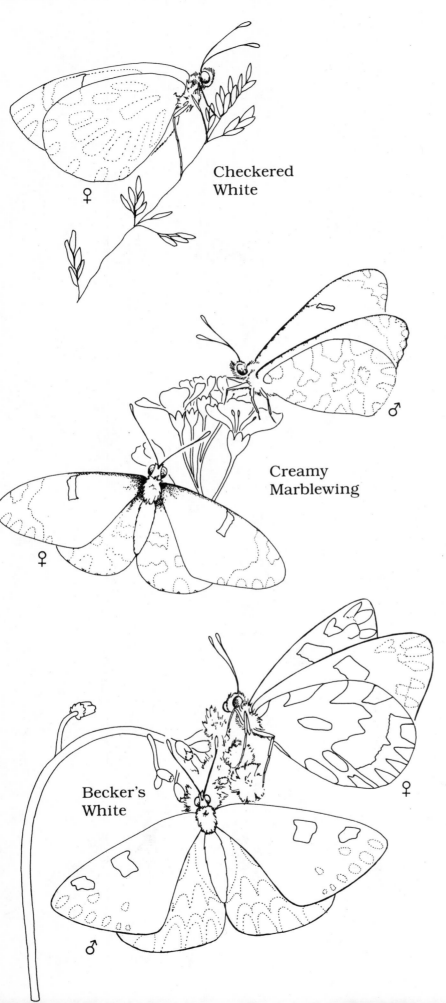

Checkered
White
♀

Creamy
Marblewing
♂

♀

Becker's
White

♀

♂

Checkered White This is a common butterfly of open spaces. Through the seasons it can vary greatly in appearance, but it always has a white base with darker markings. The females tend to be more heavily spotted than the males. On the underside, shown here, marks on the forewing are charcoal-black, while those on the hindwing are olive-green. Here it is taking nectar from spreading dogbane. (25)

Creamy Marblewing You will find this marblewing mostly in the western mountains. Above, its wings are creamy white with black markings near the tips. The underside has a lovely spring-green marbled pattern against a white background. The butterfly's large round eye is bright green, and the furry scales on its head have a greenish sheen to them. (26)

Becker's White In a hot, dry, and dusty sagebrush desert where it seems nothing is alive, this attractive butterfly is at home. Above, it is clear white with a crisp pattern of black marks; the forewing cell spot stands out as a thick black square. These spots are repeated below, along with a bold network of yellow-green scaling around the veins. (27)

Olympia Marblewing Spot this butterfly of the open plains in the Prairie Scene on p. 54. The narrow, rounded wings are linen-white, with a sparse network of marbled yellow-green bars crossing the hindwing beneath. Radiating out from the base on many individuals is a delicate rosy flush. (28)

16

Orange Sulphur A common sight in summer over much of the continent, this bright butterfly has followed the spread of alfalfa, hence its other name, Alfalfa Butterfly. Here we have a female upper side, sunny orange with yellow-spotted black borders, black spot on forewing, and a red one on the hind. The male's underside shows orangey yellow with a row of brown dots and a silver spot. Red clover is the flower. (29)

California Dogface The reason for the name is obvious in the poodle shape on the forewing of the California State Butterfly. The face shimmers with a rosy purple, surrounded by inky black. A rich shade of tangerine orange colors the hindwings. Flying Pansy is its other common name. (30)

Dwarf Yellow A remarkable migrant, also called the Dainty Sulphur, it flies northward in spring, sometimes hundreds of miles. The dark form female is pictured — lemon-yellow above with black tips and edging to the forewing, olive-green below except for orange inner forewing and dark marks. (31)

Common Sulphur A butterfly like this probably gave butterflies their name. The upperside is indeed buttery, with a coal-black margin. Below, the Common resembles the Orange Sulphur, with which it shares the alfalfa fields. Also in Butterfly Garden Scene (p. 64). (32)

Dogface Butterfly Like the California Dogface, except the poodle-heads are orange or else the whole upperside is bright yellow with black borders. With yellow forewing and green hindwing below, it resembles a leaf when at rest. Find it in the Desert Scene on p. 49. (33)

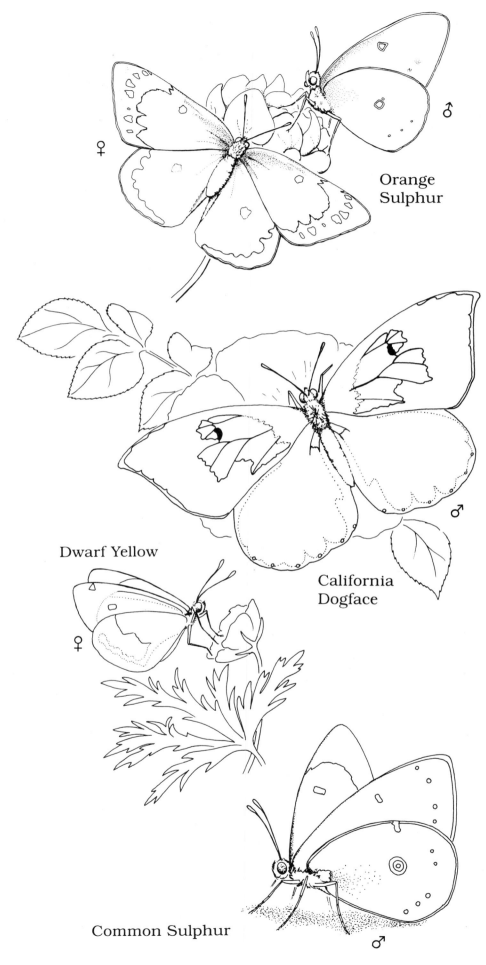

Orange
Sulphur

Dwarf Yellow

California
Dogface

Common Sulphur

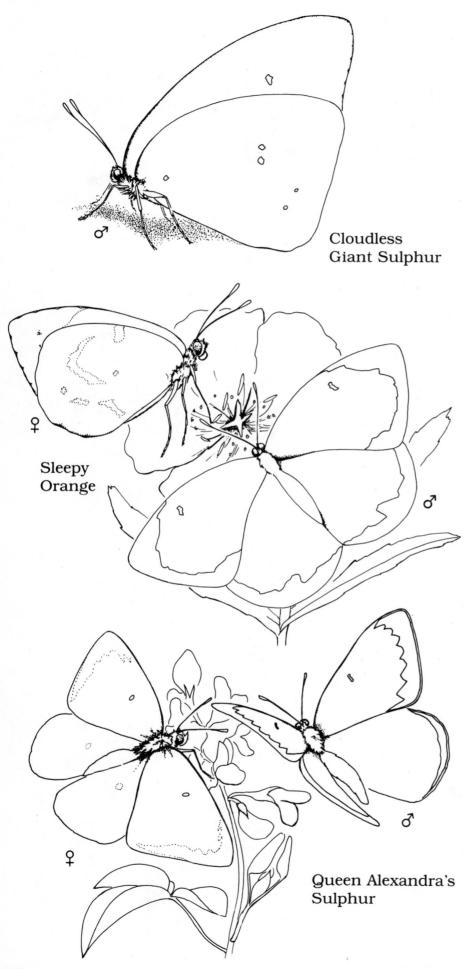

Cloudless
Giant Sulphur

Sleepy
Orange

Queen Alexandra's
Sulphur

Cloudless Giant Sulphur This big sulphur deserves the name. It is clear sulphurous yellow above. The underside has a greenish tone and varying amounts of reddish dots and speckling. Great numbers gather in the South in some years, then make mass movements toward the North. Some individuals reach destinations far beyond their breeding range. (34)

Sleepy Orange It does not act sleepy when chased, shifting into a rapid zigzag flight. Color the upperside deep burnt orange with irregular black borders. The orange carries over to the forewing below. The underside of the hindwing is golden, with rusty speckling ranging from light bands (as here) to heavy clouds. (35)

Queen Alexandra's Sulphur A sulphur of the Rockies and surrounding territories. The very bright yellow wings of the male are set off by sharp black margins. The female is a paler shade of yellow, and she has only a bit of charcoal dusting around the forewing tips. Beneath, this butterfly is colored a cool green. It perches on golden banner, a host. (36)

Pima Orangetip Shown in the Desert Scene, p. 49. The Sonoran Desert in early spring boasts a great show of wildflowers. Seeking nectar among them is the Pima, as colorful as any flower. The combination of bright yellow wings with intensely orange wingtips gives a memorable impression. The orange patches are bounded by black markings, and the hindwings are green-marbled below. (37)

Mead's Sulphur The name commemorates a pioneer lepidopterist who discovered it in Colorado. There this brilliant sulphur flies in high mountain tundra (look for it in the Alpine Scene on p. 20 also). The wings are colored deep orange with jet black borders. The eyes are green, and the furry scales around the head are bright pink, as is the fringe of the wings. Its nectar-flower is showy daisy. (38)

Tailed Orange Also called the Proterpia Orange. The tails are longer in winter generations of this southern species. The male underside, as shown, should be colored golden-orange with rusty mottling. The top edge of the forewing is banded with black above. He nectars on butterfly weed. (39)

Statira One of the tropical giant sulphurs, Statira just makes it into the southern tips of the United States. The upperside is largely yellow, with a broad white outer border. The underside is yellow, with white crossing the middle of the forewing. Sometimes seen migrating in great numbers out at sea. (40)

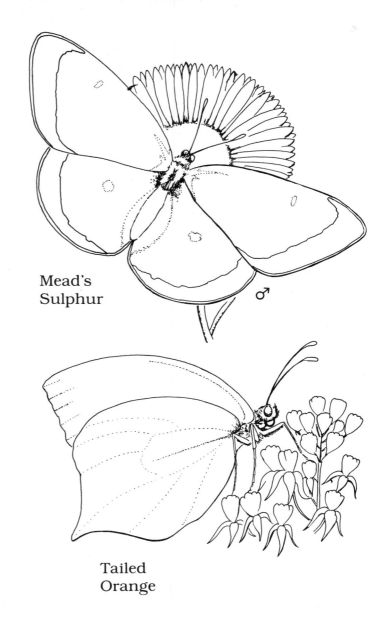

Mead's Sulphur ♂

Tailed Orange

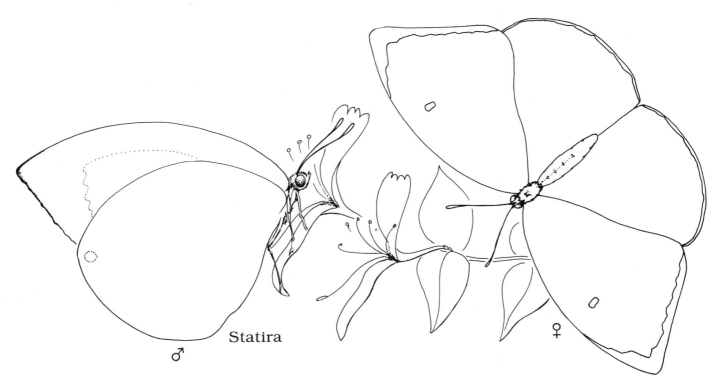

Statira ♂

♀

Alpine Scene

Orange-barred Giant Sulphur
Like its relatives, this big beauty flies speedily but dallies at flowers or to lay eggs on sennas. Make the upperside rich lemon-yellow, with a bright orange bar on the forewing. Any combination of mottled pink and orange, with pearly spots in the middle of the hindwing, may be shown by the variable underside. The female is deep yellow with black marks and an orange band across the bottom of the hindwing. (41)

Little Yellow A common immigrant from the South along the East Coast, the Little Yellow is found in all kinds of open places. This mating pair show their undersides — yellow with some black overscaling, rusty smudges, and a sooty mark near the upper edge of the hindwing. (42)

White Angled Sulphur A very large, unique butterfly, also called Clorinde. It is resident in Texas but strays northward. The broad wings are like white cotton sheets. Each has a black spot in the cell, ringed with red. A bright yellow bar stands out on the forewing, extending from the upper edge toward the middle. (43)

Alpine Scene (p. 20)

A surprising variety of butterflies has adapted to the harsh environment where the tundra meets the rockslide above timberline. During the brief high-country summer in the Rockies, male Phoebus Parnassians (14) seek females over their host plant, yellow stonecrop. Mead's Sulphur (38) and the High Mountain Blue (81) sail on the thin air. Rockslide specialists, the Lustrous Copper (72) basks on a boulder and the Magdalena Alpine (172) visits pink campion.

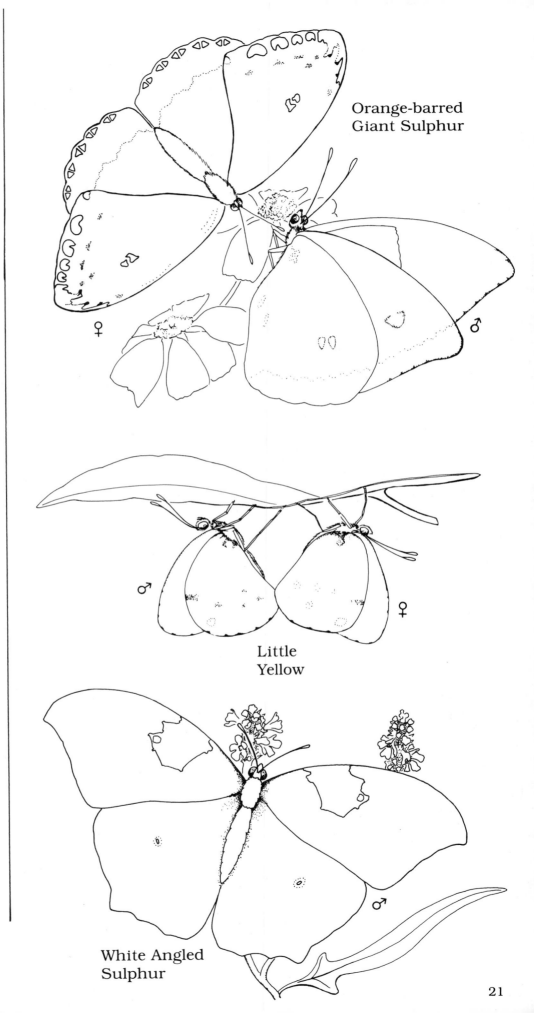

Orange-barred
Giant Sulphur

Little
Yellow

White Angled
Sulphur

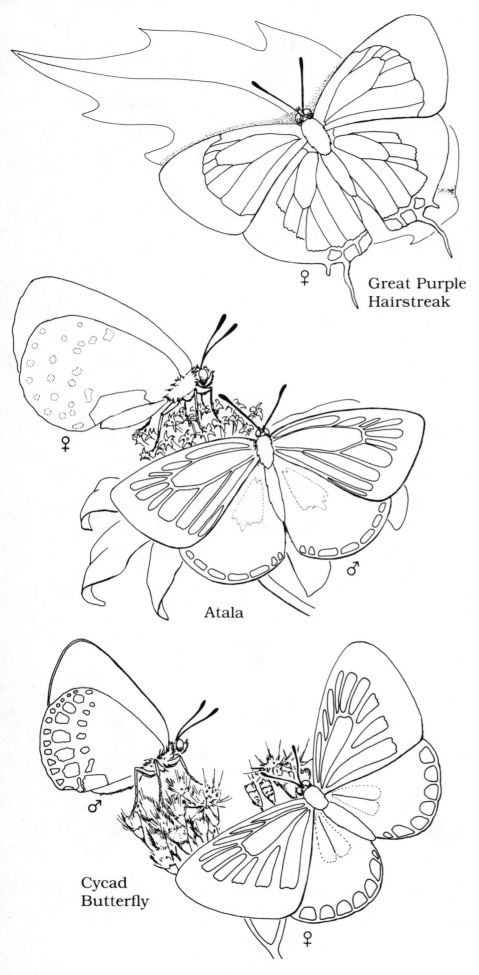

Great Purple
Hairstreak
♀

Atala
♀
♂

Cycad
Butterfly
♂
♀

Gossamer-winged Butterflies

Mostly small and fast-flying, the gossamer wings tend toward metallic colors and iridescence. The Gossamer Wing family (Lycaenidae) includes hairstreaks and elfins, coppers, blues, the carnivorous Harvester, and the metalmarks (sometimes put in their own family, Riodinidae). Most people overlook these tiny fliers, but they are well worth paying attention to for their brilliance and fascinating behavior.

Great Purple Hairstreak   Its other name, Great Blue Hairstreak, may be more suitable. The upperside is the deepest, most brilliant iridescent blue, on the body as well as the wings. A black border outlines the wings and greenish reflections may show, especially in the spots near the long tails. Our largest hairstreak. Its caterpillars feed on mistletoe, parasites of oak trees. (44)

Atala   A beautiful Bahamian butterfly. Once common in Florida, Atala became nearly extinct in the United States due to habitat changes and development. Just a few small colonies are known now, where the larvae feed on coontie. On the underside, the wings are matte black with several rows of sapphire blue spots and a large fire-engine red spot that extends onto the abdomen as well. The upperside is black on the edges and veins, otherwise bright shiny green with a green thorax and red abdomen. (45)

Cycad Butterfly   This close cousin of Atala looks like it except for having more black above, the iridescence bluer green, and the hindwing row of spots lime green. Beneath, the fringe and spots are blue-green, except for the red patch and abdomen. Seen in North America only in Texas. (46)

Early Hairstreak Famous for its rarity and mystery. Some collectors believe it lives mostly in the canopy of the eastern hardwood forest. The basic color beneath is a cool bluish green. All of the spots as well as the wing fringes are brick-red with white edges. (47)

Silver-banded Hairstreak Sometimes called Sarita. The chartreuse wings are crossed by silvery-white bands. Farther out there is a wavy chestnut brown area, next a row of frosty brown patches, finally the white wing fringes and white-tipped brown tails. (48)

Bramble Green Hairstreak One of a number of green hairstreaks in the West. The wings below are bright apple green with a warm brown band across the forewing and small white spots on the hindwing. Caterpillars feed on lotus and buckwheat, become butterflies in springtime. (49)

Olive Hairstreak Here is a hairstreak of the East, often common around its host, red cedars. The complex pattern of the underside involves a bright olive-green background crossed by rows of clear white bars. Regions around the bars are reddish brown, and the outer band of spots is frosty. (50)

Nelson's Hairstreak Different groups of Nelson's Hairstreaks feed on different western cedars and may be separate species. Their coloration varies also. The one depicted here is deep purplish with a flush of rusty through much of the forewing, white bars, black dots, frosty margin of the hindwing. (51)

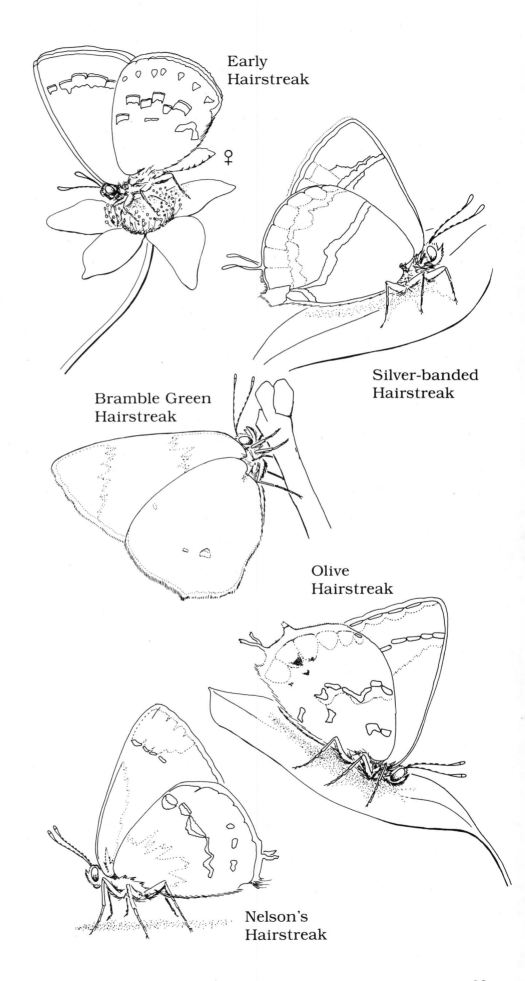

Early
Hairstreak

Silver-banded
Hairstreak

Bramble Green
Hairstreak

Olive
Hairstreak

Nelson's
Hairstreak

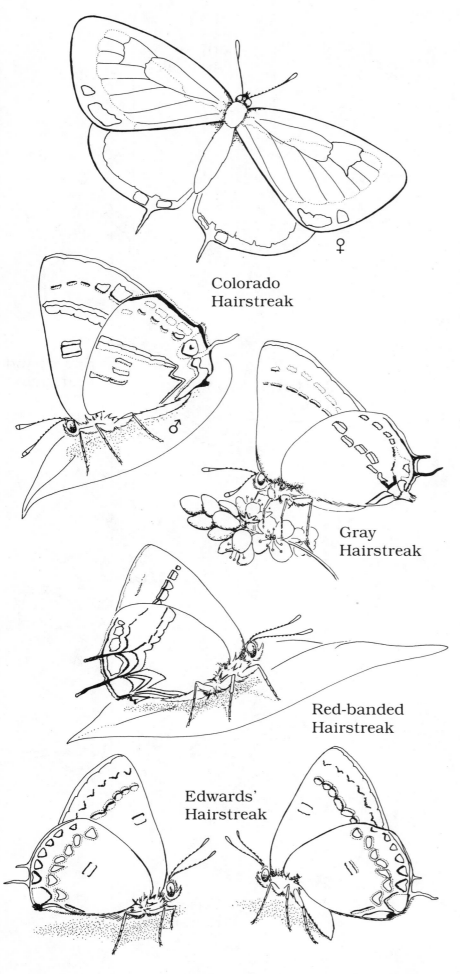

Colorado
Hairstreak

Gray
Hairstreak

Red-banded
Hairstreak

Edwards'
Hairstreak

Colorado Hairstreak   A large, spectacular hairstreak, the Colorado darts around scrub oaks in the Southwest. Deep amythest purple covers the upperside except for black margins, a black bar outside the forewing cell and bright orange spots in the corner of each wing. The underside is warm gray-brown, crossed by black-edged white bands, with orange spots and a band of sky blue around the outer edge. (52)

Gray Hairstreak   Common countrywide, with a broad diet from hops to beans. The wings range from a clear, dove gray to dark slate gray, above and below. Rows of white bars are edged inwardly with black. Just in from each tail lies a red-orange spot with a black pupil. The tails and bright spot distract birds from the head and body of the hairstreak. (53)

Red-banded Hairstreak   This pretty hairstreak abounds in the South. Gray-brown wings are crossed by a broad red band, lined with white and with white hoops in the thickest red part. Black spots run around the rim, and the one between the tails is often ringed with red. A blue patch lies below the longer tail. (54)

Edwards' Hairstreak   Here two of these active butterflies are jostling for territory. Most of the wing surface is tan, and most of the markings are black with white edges. Inside the fringe a row of red-orange diamonds runs down to the tails. Below the tails shine a sky-blue patch and a bright red streak. (55)

Eastern Pine Elfin Like a very similar western species, this elfin feeds as a caterpillar on pine needles. The colors below are different shades of brown and gray, with white streaks. Brown triangles point inward from the frosted and checkered margins. (56)

Henry's Elfin Although quite widespread in the East, this little butterfly is not common. It is strongly two-toned below. The inner part of the hindwing is chocolate, that of the forewing cinnamon, and the outer half of both is toasty brown. (57)

Moss Elfin This western elfin was named for a man named Moss, but it also frequents mossy balds and outcrops. The caterpillars feed on stonecrop. The inner part of the wings is dark brown, the outer part reddish brown, margin white. On pearly everlasting. (58)

Bog Elfin Occurs in moist, peaty places with Bog Coppers and Bog Fritillaries. The zigzag markings below are smudged, and dark brown patches alternate with cocoa bands. White scales run through the middle and margin of the underside. Nectaring on pearly everlasting. (59)

Brown Elfin Both the larvae and adults like blueberry flowers. Common in many kinds of places over much of the land, Brown Elfins vary in color. This one is dark brown above and mahogany, reddish brown, below. The inner half is darker than the outer part. (60)

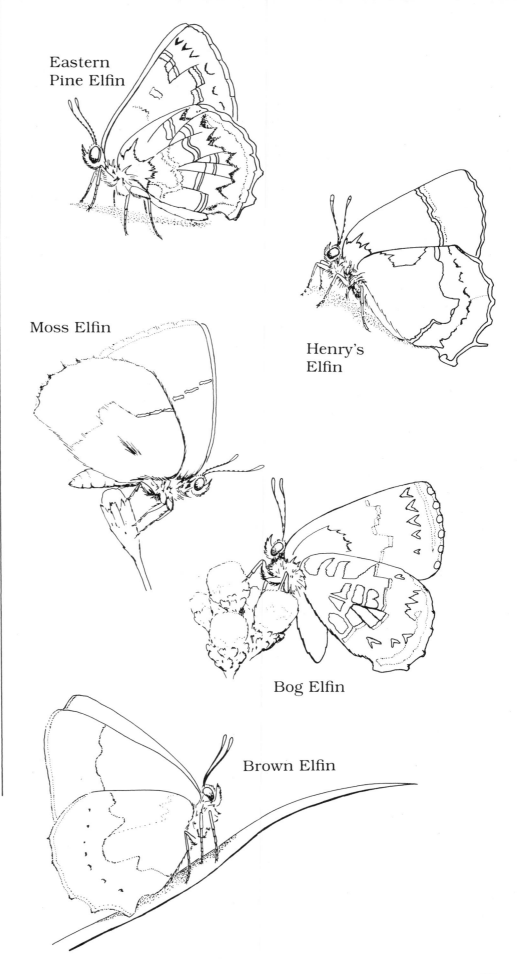

Eastern Pine Elfin

Henry's Elfin

Moss Elfin

Bog Elfin

Brown Elfin

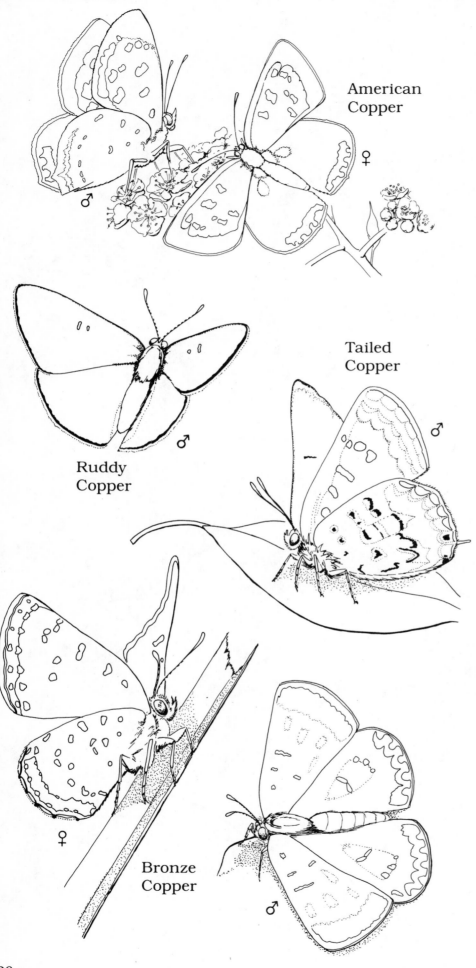

American Copper

Tailed Copper

Ruddy Copper

Bronze Copper

American Copper Despite its name, also found in Europe. Known as the Small Copper in England. The forewing above is fiery orange with dark brown spots and borders. The pattern is reversed on the hindwing, with red spots and bands against dusky brown. The coloration beneath is similar except the orange is paler and the brown lighter and grayer with inky black spots. (61)

Ruddy Copper The most brilliant of our coppers is wholly copper except for tiny black dots and narrow black and white margins. The female is duller and spottier. As it flies, the male Ruddy flashes copper and silver because the underside is silky white. The western half of North America is its domain. (62)

Tailed Copper Basking with the wings partly open, as shown here, is a common posture for coppers. This species has orange tails with orange and black markings next to them, like hairstreaks. This male's upper forewing is brown. The underside has alternating bands of cream and cocoa-color, and a broad orange streak through the forewing. (63)

Bronze Copper Color the upperside deep brown with purplish highlights, black dots, and a flaming orange zigzag band around the edge of the hindwings. The orange border repeats below, and the dots are black, against the silvery white hindwing and the clear, pale orange forewing with its light gray edge. Also to be found in the Eastern Swamp (p. 13), a favorite habitat. (64)

Harvester Not truly a copper but a relative, the Harvester has a unique life history. Its caterpillars prey upon certain woolly aphids. The adults may visit the aphids also for honey-dew. The irregular, interior area of the forewings and the lower halves of the hindwings are pumpkin orange; the rest is black, with thin white fringes. (65)

Blue Copper Bluer than any true blue, yet its wing veins and other structures prove it to be an unusual kind of copper. With the exception of the thin white fringe and black border, the male's entire upper surface shimmers metallic blue. You can give it greenish and silvery highlights, which are the effects of prismlike scales. Strictly a western butterfly. (66)

Nivalis Copper A very good alternative name is the Lilac-bordered Copper. This refers to the broad, irregular band of soft lilac-purple that surrounds the underside of the hindwing. Orange crescents run through the lilac field. The remainder of the lower surface is a rich orangey yellow, with black spots. Nivalis refers to snow — it is an insect of cool western mountains. (67)

Gorgon Copper This California Copper is associated with wild buckwheats, as are many gossamer-winged butterflies. While the male is purplish brown, the female shown here has a complicated pattern of pale yellow-orange, black spots, and dusky brown borders and patches. Light orange hoops run along the lower margin of the hindwing. She nectars on false dandelion. (68)

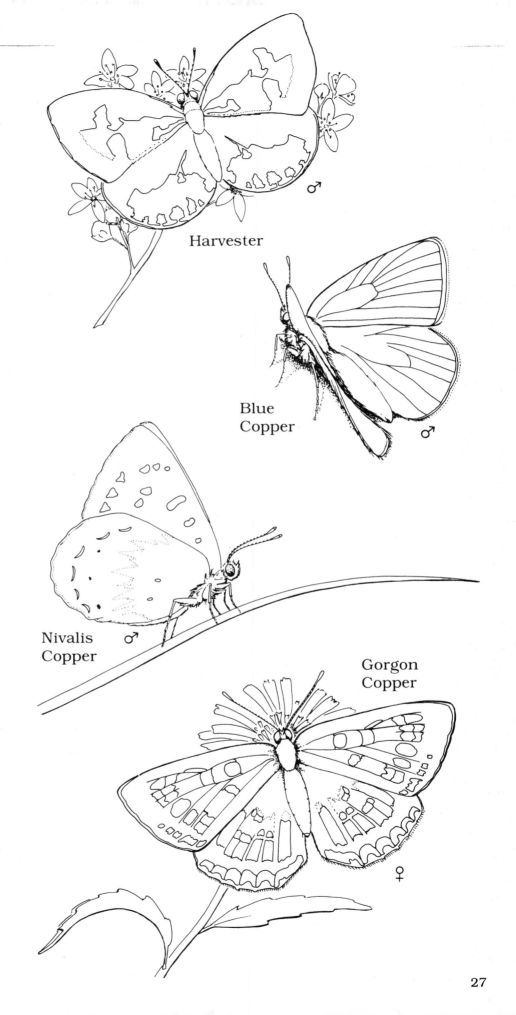

Harvester

Blue Copper

Nivalis Copper

Gorgon Copper

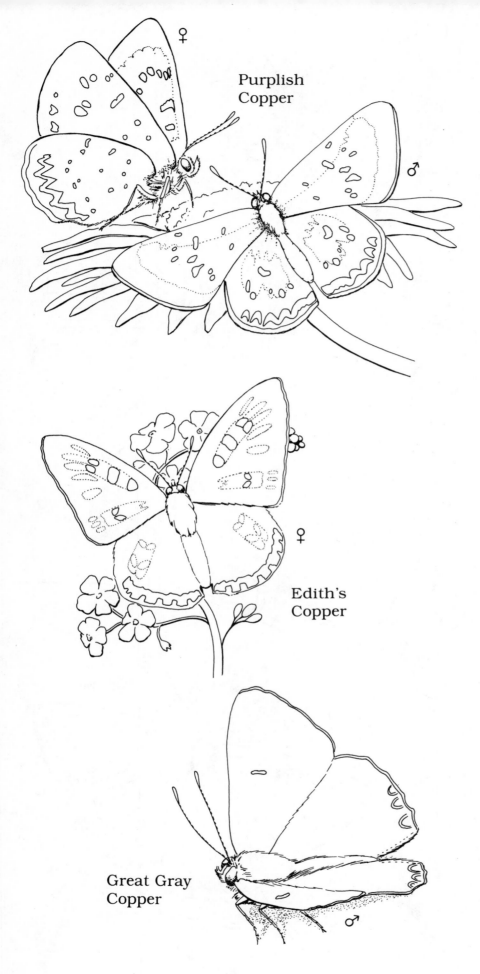

Purplish
Copper

Edith's
Copper

Great Gray
Copper

Purplish Copper In the right light, the brown wings of the male shine with a stunning iridescent purple. Forewing borders are brown, the hindwing edging is orange and dots are black. The underside of the hindwing is cocoa-brown with orange zigzags, the forewing light orange, with brown dots over all. This is a common, adaptable species whose larvae feed on docks. The adults visit flowers like balsamroot. (69)

Edith's Copper Edith was the sweetheart of an early lepidopterist, who named this pretty butterfly for her. It lives in the West, occurring in both Yellowstone and Yosemite. The female, shown here, is dusky brown with pale orange patches bearing black spots. A pale orange pattern encircles the bottom edge of the hindwing. She is probing forget-me-not. (70)

Great Gray Copper Except for a black dot on the forewing, a touch of orange on the hindwing crescents, and the thin white fringe, the Great Gray Copper is just what the name says. The shade of gray is dark and brownish. Most abundant in the Midwest, this impressive copper likes watercourses and milkweed flowers. (71)

Lustrous Copper This very metallic and bright little copper appears in the Alpine Scene on p. 20. It is one of a number of butterflies that occur mostly on high mountain rockslides, above timberline. It is all clear, fiery orange-copper except for black dots and a black border with a white fringe. (72)

Orange-veined Blue Not really blue but deep brown, its veins lined with coppery orange scales. A broad orange band along the lower part of the hindwings has black spots running into the blackish border, itself surrounded by a pale fringe. Found only in the mountains of Southern California. (73)

Spring Azure Here is a favorite herald of spring. Shown is an early-season female, deep violet-blue with prominent black borders on the forewings and marginal spots on the hindwings. As with many blues, its fringe is whitish. Since its caterpillars accept buds and flowers of many kinds of native shrubs, the Spring Azure occurs very widely. Here she examines Indian plum. Also shown in the Butterfly Garden (p. 64). (74)

Eastern Tailed Blue A western species exists also. In both, the wings are the clearest deep silvery blue above on the males, though the female is gray. This male also shows black spots around the edge, the one nearest the little tail being orange-capped. Beneath, the color is light gray, with spots of charcoal and two of orange by the tail. The body, fringe, and tails are white. Look for it around clover. (75)

Acmon Blue Also known as the Emerald-studded Blue, because of shiny green-blue spots on the underside. This one is a male, bright blue with black borders. Broad, wavy, orange bands with black spots line the hindwings. A widespread buckwheat feeder. (76)

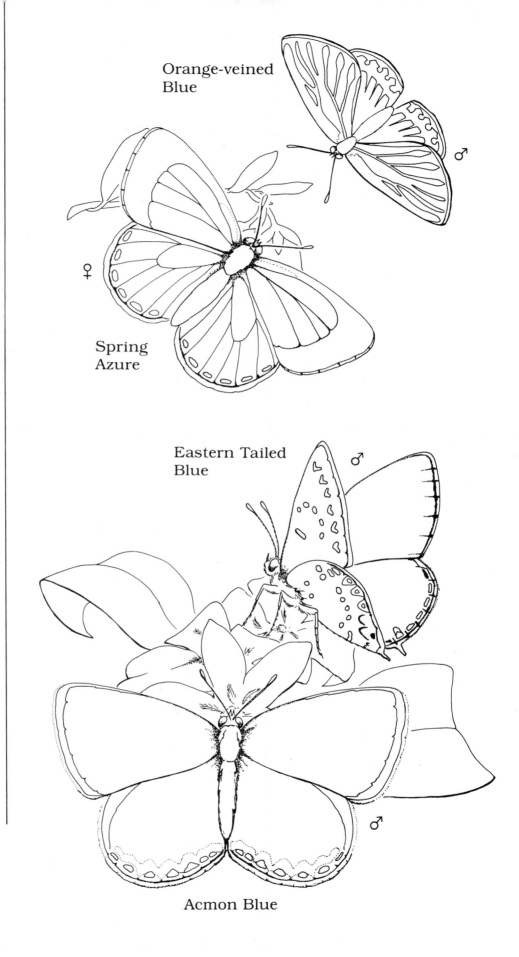

Orange-veined Blue

Spring Azure

Eastern Tailed Blue

Acmon Blue

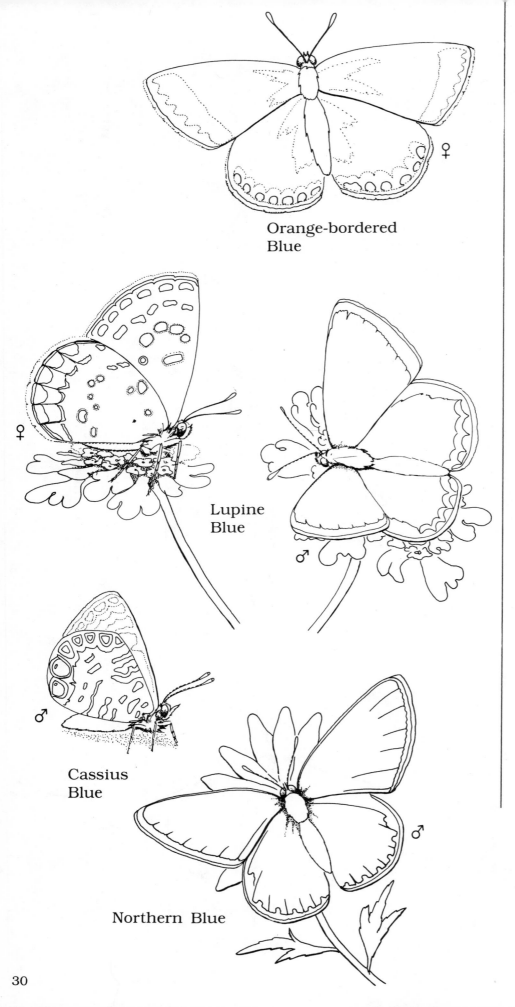

Orange-bordered
Blue

Lupine
Blue

♀

♂

Cassius
Blue

♂

Northern Blue

♂

Orange-bordered Blue The black body and brown wings of this female are speckled with metallic blue scales. Orange borders are scalloped with brown dots, edged by a white fringe. It is also called the Melissa Blue, and a famous endangered race in New York State is known as the Karner Blue. (77)

Lupine Blue Despite its name, this blue's host plant is wild buckwheat, yellow-flowered with pale green leaves. The silvery gray underside has black spots, orange hoops with black caps enclosing gemlike blue dots. The iridescent blue upperside is black-margined and white-fringed with orange hoops. (78)

Cassius Blue The pattern of this Deep Southern wanderer is a complicated interplay of gray-brown and cream. The two largest spots are black with blue centers and orange rims. (79)

Northern Blue This mountain-loving blue gets its name from its range around the Northern Hemisphere. It haunts trailsides and creeks, nectaring as shown here on yellow wild daisies and other wildflowers. Color it deep indigo blue with a narrow black border and white fringe and body fur. (80)

High Mountain Blue Spot this high country and arctic species in the Alpine Scene on p. 20. Above, it is colored gray-brown, shot with pale blue, while the warm gray underside has outstanding white spots. Fringes white, borders and discal spot black. (81)

Sonoran Blue A light shiny blue uniquely marked with orange patches on fore- and hindwings, black spots and checkered fringes. It occurs in the mountains and deserts of California and Baja California. Memorable for its lovely pattern. (82)

Blackburn's Bluet Also known as the Hawaiian Blue, this is one of only two butterflies native to those islands. The pure grass-green underside and contrasting deep blue upperside with black edging make it very striking in flight but hard to spot at rest. (83)

Greenish Blue The name comes from the male, whose bright blue wings have greenish reflections. Here we have a female, showing her soft brown, black-dotted underside. She perches on white clover, a frequent host plant. (84)

Shasta Blue Another female. Her wings are dark coppery brown with white fringes and orange zigzags, and with bright blue scales invading from the blue furry thorax outward. Shasta Blues fly high in the Sierra Nevada and the Rockies, on prairies too, but not much in between. (85)

Silvery Blue Among the very bluest of blues, the Silvery flies over much of the continent. Found in many habitats, but we have placed it in the Prairie Scene on p. 54. A light, sky blue with metallic highlights, black edge, white fuzzy fringe. (86)

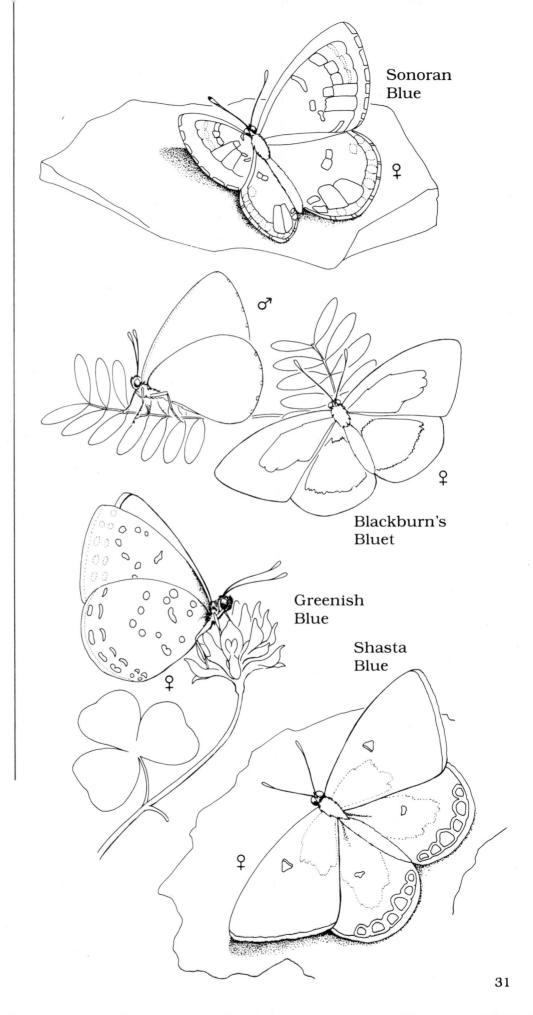

Sonoran
Blue
♀

♂

♀

Blackburn's
Bluet

Greenish
Blue

Shasta
Blue

♀

♀

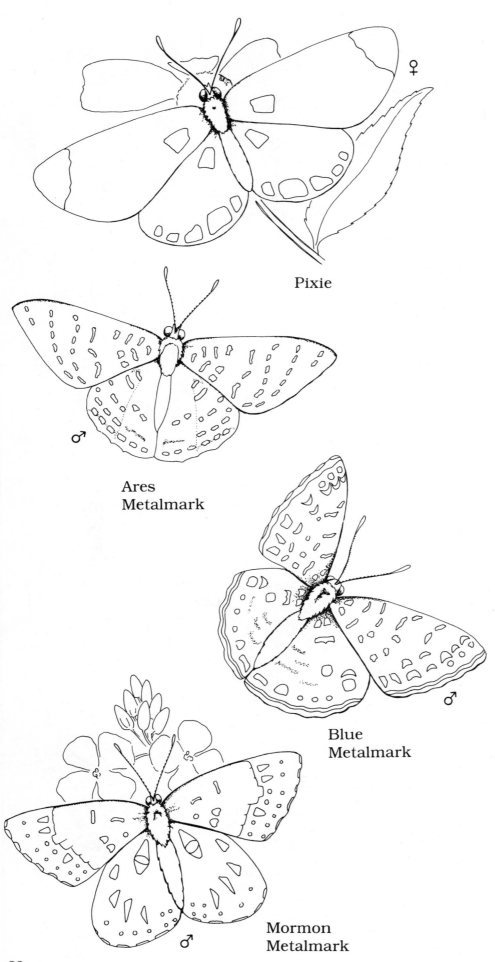

Pixie

Ares
Metalmark

Blue
Metalmark

Mormon
Metalmark

Pixie The Pixie does not look like the other metalmarks, yet it belongs with them. Mostly jet black, it sports a bright red spot near the base of each wing, a row of scarlet around the hindwings, and yellow forewing tips. A Texan. (87)

Ares Metalmark The metalmarks are often put in their own family, the Riodinidae. Ares is brown with black spots, its hindwings orange-flushed. It flies in the Southwest, and like other metalmarks, it often perches with its wings outspread. (88)

Blue Metalmark This tropical butterfly barely reaches South Texas. Its body and wings are metallic blue with black bars and spots, and its eyes are yellow. The white fringe is checkered with black. (89)

Mormon Metalmark A bright little butterfly of drier parts of the American West. It varies greatly, but this is typical — dark brown, banded with deep orange, spotted and checkered with clear white. Here it is visiting western wallflower. Another favorite nectar source is the larval host plant, wild buckwheat. (90)

Swamp Metalmark Spot it in the scene of an Eastern Swamp, its preferred habitat (p. 13). One of three northeastern metalmark species, it shows the group's typical metallic silvery bars. Otherwise, rusty brown crossed by rows of dark brown dots and marks. (91)

Brush-footed Butterflies

The Nymphalidae is the largest and most diverse butterfly family, numerous all over the world. They range from small to large, and most are bright and colorful with striking patterns. Some, such as tortoiseshells, hibernate through the winter as adults; others migrate. Traditionally, milkweeds (including the Monarch), longwings, and snouts have been placed in separate families (Danaidae, Heliconidae, and Libytheidae), but they all have the tiny forelegs that give the family its name and show other signs that they are related.

Baltimore The official State Butterfly of Maryland, much beloved by butterfly watchers. Black wings have red-orange spots near the base and all around the edges, white spots and crescents in between. The turtlehead it perches on is the caterpillar's favorite food plant. (92)

Gillette's Checkerspot There are several checkerspots in the West, all variable and confusing to identify except this one. Its broad, orange-red bands alternating with rows of white spots and black filling make its appearance unique. Yellowstone and Grand Teton national parks are good places to look for it. (93)

Leanira Males and mountain forms are darker than females and checkerspots of the dry basin and range country of the West. The male's ground color is dark brown, its spots vanilla except for the outermost ones, which are orange. Orange bars near the forewing tip. The female's underside forewing is light orange, with yellow spots; the hindwing shows a black chain and veins against a creamy yellow background. (94)

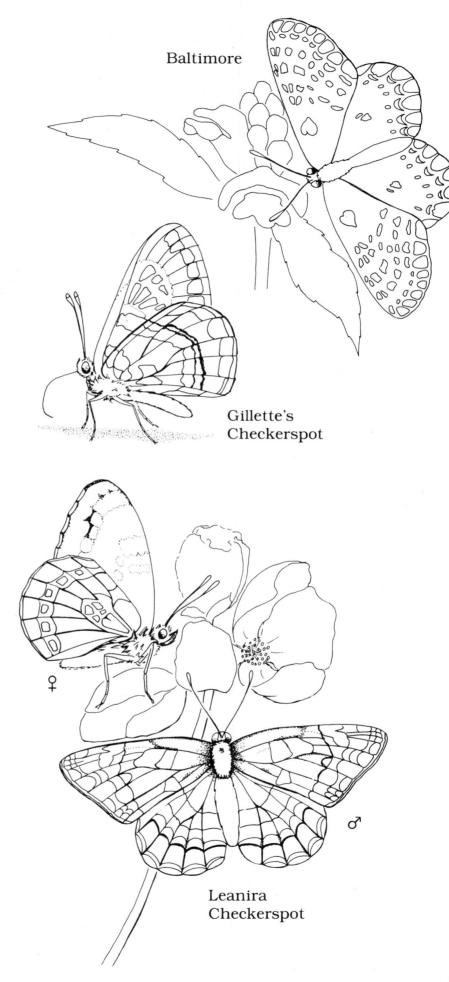

Baltimore

Gillette's
Checkerspot

♀

♂

Leanira
Checkerspot

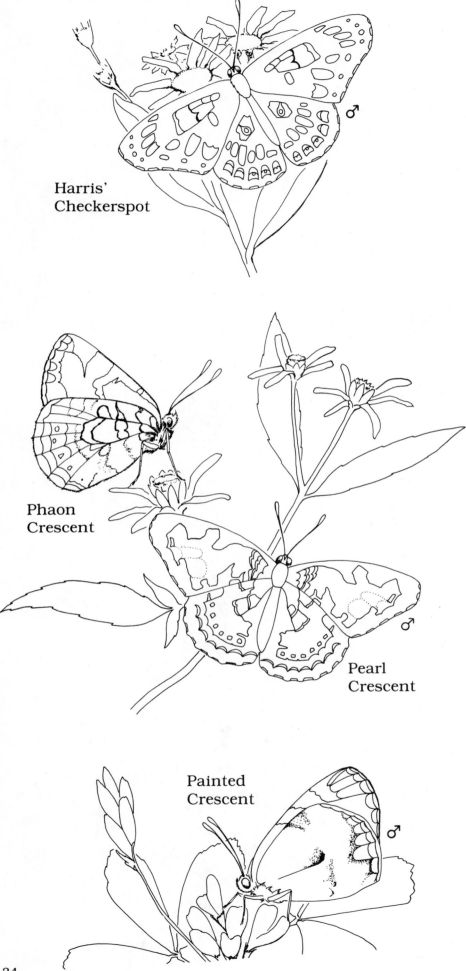

**Harris'
Checkerspot**

**Phaon
Crescent**

**Pearl
Crescent**

**Painted
Crescent**

Harris' Checkerspot This northeastern checker haunts moist meadows with irises and asters. Here it visits aster, its host plant. The butterfly has broad black borders, orange spot-bands across the middle, and black and orange networks near the base. May be numerous. (95)

Phaon Crescent Crescents are so-called because of a pale crescent-shaped marking along the outer edge of the hindwing below. You can see this mark on the Phaon, perched on a favorite nectar source, beggar's tick. The rest of the hindwing is pale cheesy colored with brown marks and orange spots. The forewing is orange with black and yellow patches. (96)

Pearl Crescent A most familiar butterfly, known for its habit of flying out at other insects. It likes to visit mud and flowers. Here it takes nectar from showy daisy. The amount of blackish marking varies with sex and season, but the open orange middles of the wings typify most Pearl Crescents. Watch for it in sunny, flowery places all summer long. (97)

Painted Crescent Visiting alfalfa for nectar, this one reveals its underside. The hindwing is pale, clear yellow with dark mark by the crescent. Forewing orange painted with black and white patches and a yellow tip. These bright crescents fly along ditches and roadsides, laying their eggs on asters. (98)

Janais Patch The black wings of the Janais Patch hold a small galaxy of white spots. On the hindwings, great scarlet patches show. Like many other butterflies resident in Mexico and farther south, the Janais Patch colonizes southern Texas until a cold winter drives it back. Yellow and pink lantana attracts many butterflies to its sweet nectar, including this bright patch. (99)

Definite Patch Patches are checkerspots, and this one is certainly checkered. The forewing has orange spots alternating with black, and a row of white dots along the edge. Black lines encircle the white spots and bigger red patches on the hindwings. The Definite Patch lives in thorny places in the Southwest. (100)

Bordered Patch Also known by the name of Scudder's Patched Butterfly. Widespread and common in the southwestern states and Mexico. This patch looks very different from place to place. The one shown here is a female from Texas, visiting a favorite food plant, sunflower. Color her borders black with an outer row of yellow spots, an inner row of white dots; then a broad area of fiery orange, and black bases with orange spots. Shown again in Desert Scene (p. 49). (101)

Janais Patch

Definite Patch

Bordered Patch

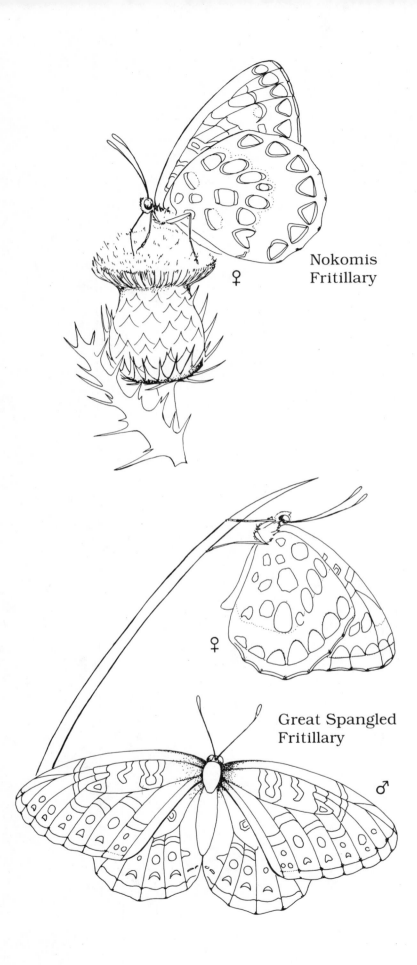

Nokomis
Fritillary

♀

Great Spangled
Fritillary

♀

♂

Nokomis Fritillary A big, rather rare fritillary of the southwestern mountains. Since it occurs around moisture in generally arid areas, drainage and water diversion threaten the survival of Nokomis. This is a female, taking nectar from a thistle — a favorite activity of fritillaries. Her wings are olive green, banded with pale yellow toward the outside. The spots in rows are shining silver, and the forewing is flushed with pink at the base. (102)

Great Spangled Fritillary The male here shows his upper-side, the female her under, as they nectar on scarlet cardinal flower. The male should be colored brilliant golden-orange, with his intricate pattern of spots done in black. The female's hindwing is rich reddish brown with a yellow outer band, the "spangles" being the silvered spots scattered across the wing and running around its rim. This common eastern species is a great favorite with butterfly gardeners. (103)

Regal Fritillary The largest fritillary is also one of the most specialized. Its preference for virgin prairies has made it rare, as these have been disturbed in the Great Plains and eastward. You may find it in the nature reserve depicted in the Prairie Scene on p. 54. Perching with its wings closed, it shows an olive hindwing spattered with big silver spots. The forewing is very bright orange with black marks and more silver around its edges. (104)

Edwards' Fritillary The name commemorates a great pioneer American lepidopterist. This is another large fritillary of the West. Like other fritillaries, its larvae feed only on violets. Adults, like this one, love to visit purple horsemint. The underside is chiefly bluish green, studded with big, metallic silver orbs. Toward its base, the forewing has a pretty pink flush. (105)

Variegated Fritillary Not a true fritillary, the Variegated lacks silver spots. Its name refers to a complex pattern of brown, white, and orange scaling on the underside. Frosty white areas and veins run through the tan base color, while the inner part of the forewing is bright orange. Eyespots bluish-black. The caterpillars eat many kinds of plants, unlike most butterflies. Every spring this resident of the South populates the northern states, only to die back with the frosts of autumn. (106)

Diana Named for the Greek goddess of the woods, Diana is one of the most strikingly dimorphic butterflies. That is, the males and females look entirely different. Here the male pursues the female on the wing. He is fiery orange beyond a large coal-black wingbase. She has the same black middle part, but outside of it has pale bluish spots on the forewing and deep blue patches and bars on the hindwing. That blue coloration, unique among fritillaries, evolved to help her mimic the poisonous Pipevine Swallowtail. That way birds will leave her alone. (107)

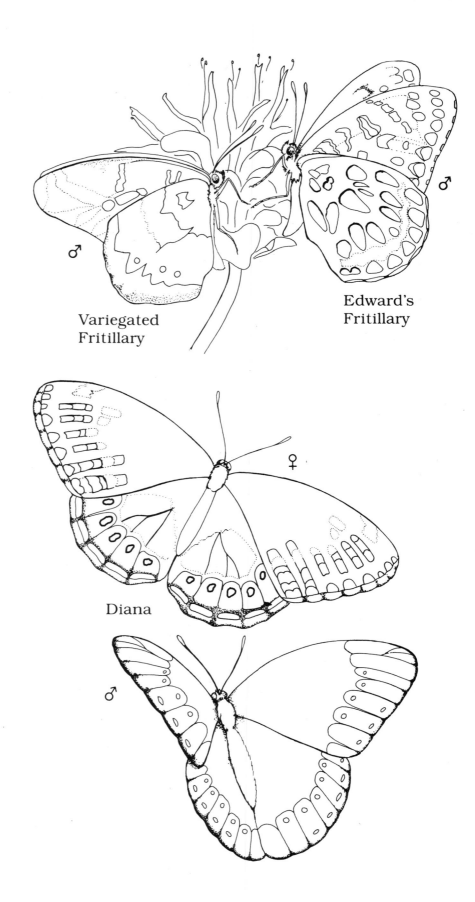

Variegated
Fritillary

Edward's
Fritillary

Diana

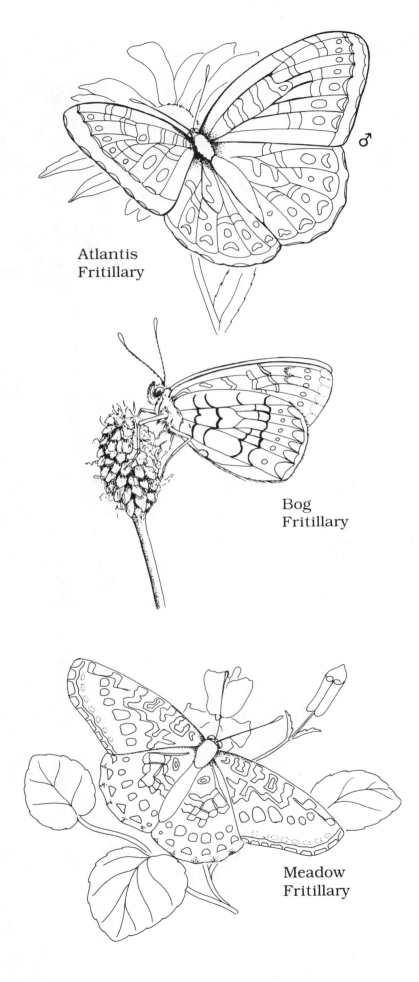

Atlantis
Fritillary

Bog
Fritillary

Meadow
Fritillary

Atlantis Fritillary As with most of the fritillaries, there is a great deal of variation in the Atlantis from place to place. This species ranges across the northern part of the country. Eastern individuals will sometimes visit gardens, attracted by black-eyed Susans or other flowers. It is difficult to draw but simple to color: the border and all the spots are black, otherwise it is all pumpkin-orange. (108)

Bog Fritillary This and the next two kinds represent the lesser fritillaries. Many of them live in bogs, but especially this one. The forewing is pale orange with black marks and two rows of yellow spots. These rows carry over onto the hindwing, where bands of pale yellow alternate with bands of brick red. It sits on plantain. (109)

Meadow Fritillary The snipped-off-looking tip of the forewings gives the best clue to this species. Colored like other fritillaries, light orange with black markings. A denizen of wet meadows, East and West. This one is visiting a violet, on which the caterpillars feed and the adults may take nectar. (110)

Silver-bordered Fritillary Another widespread fritillary of bogs and meadows, this one lives in Europe as well. It is a lesser fritillary, but like the greater fritillaries it possesses silver spots on its underside. These alternate with rows of reddish brown and tawny. This fritillary is shown with other butterflies of the eastern swamp on p. 13 (111)

Queen The milkweed butterflies, represented here by the Queen and the Monarch, are often put in their own family (Danaidae). The Queen has rich cinnamon wings with black borders and clusters of small white spots. The black patches on the hindwings produce chemical perfumes, and show that this individual is a male. He is visiting milkweed for nectar, the same plant he fed on as a caterpillar. In Florida, Viceroys have evolved a dark race to mimic Queens. (112)

Monarch Surely our best known North American butterfly, yet still holding many mysteries. The bright orange Monarch has black veins and borders, with white spots around the edges and peach-colored patches in the black forewing tip area. The common milkweed it is visiting also nourishes the larvae and makes the Monarch poisonous to birds. Viceroys mimic Monarchs, so birds ignore them as well. Monarchs breed all across the continent, but in the autumn they migrate like birds. Great numbers fly to Mexico or to California, where they spend the winter in huge clusters among the foliage of trees. Then in spring they return to the breeding grounds again. Also in Butterfly Garden, p. 64. (113)

Crimson-patched Longwing. The longwings too are considered by some scientists to be in a different family (called Heliconidae) from the brush-footed butterflies. They live in the American tropics and feed on passion flowers. This kind is sometimes found in Texas. Here it nectars on lantana. Jet black, the forewings have crimson patches, hindwings a yellow streak along the top. (114)

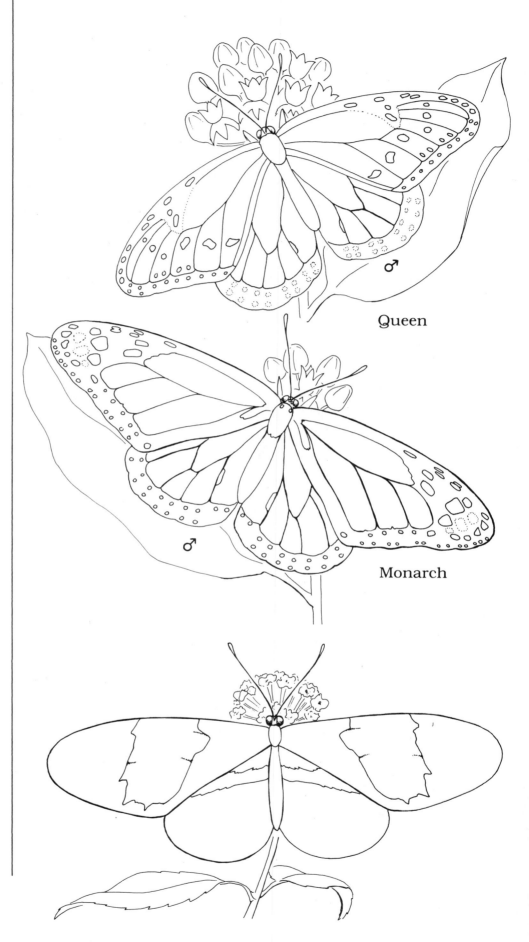

Queen

Monarch

Crimson-patched Longwing

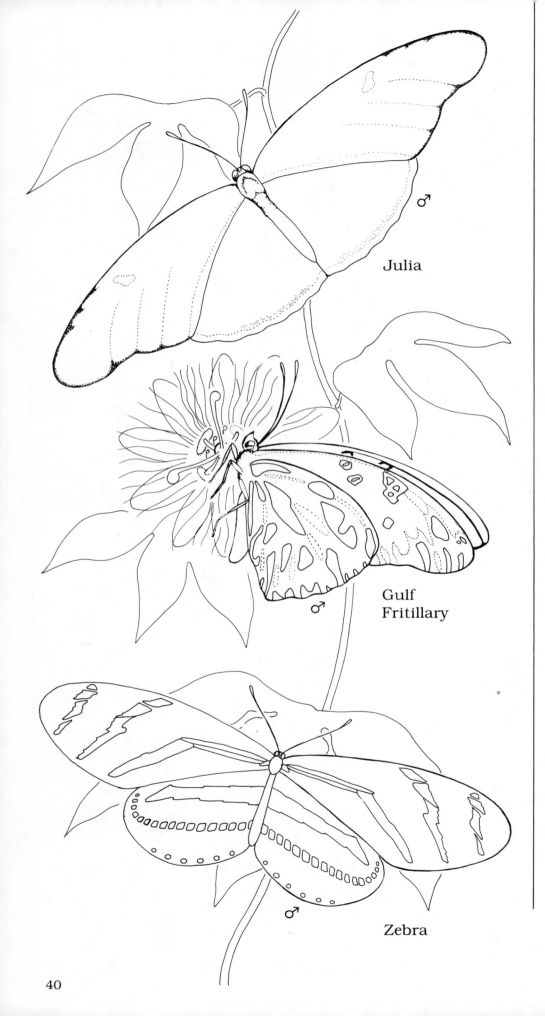

Julia

Gulf
Fritillary

Zebra

Julia The long wings of Julia are almost entirely clear, deep orange above, except for a black spot along the upper edge. The body is clothed in furry orange scales. All the butterflies on this page feed on passion flower vines as caterpillars. Julia lives in southern Texas and Florida, where she swarms sometimes. (115)

Gulf Fritillary This longwing is called a fritillary because like those butterflies it has brilliant metallic silver spots beneath. On the hindwing and the tip of the forewing, these are set in a field of olive-gold. The rest of the forewing changes to crimson-pink. Common across the South and all around the Gulf of Mexico, it loves flowers such as beggar's tick and lantana. (116)

Zebra This southeastern longwing haunts hammocks in the Everglades. Common where passion flower vines grow in woody spots, even in towns. A wonderful sight is to see a number of Zebras gathering in a tree for their evening's roost together. The color scheme is a simple one: yellow stripes and spots against a black velvety background. (117)

Southeastern Woods Scene *(p. 41)*

The mixed hardwoods of the Southeast comprise one of our richest butterfly habitats. The big Palamedes Swallowtail (4) likes watersides. The blue female Diana (107), flying, is mimicked by the Red-spotted Purple (122), here nectaring on scarlet cardinal flower and showing its brick-red spots. Meanwhile, a Pearly Eye (156) rests on a grass blade and a Whirlabout (181) skipper basks on a stone.

107

156

122

181

4

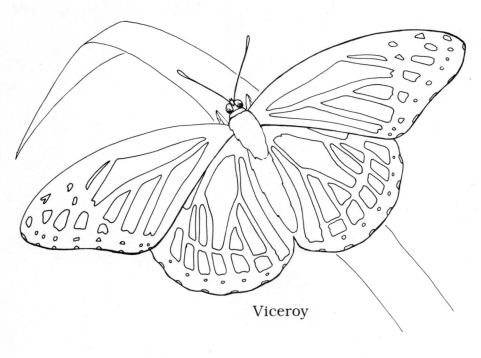

Viceroy

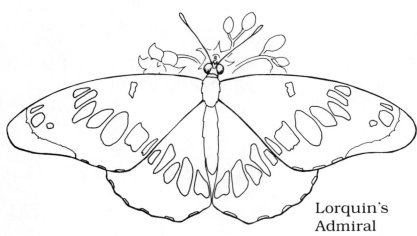

Lorquin's
Admiral

Viceroy Although not closely related, the Viceroy looks very much like the Monarch. This gives it protection from birds that have learned to avoid the distasteful Monarchs. Its deep orange color, black veins and borders, and white dots are like those of the Monarch, but it also has a black line around the hindwing past the middle. Look for Viceroys around willows, especially along watercourses. Its close relatives are the banded admirals. (118)

Lorquin's Admiral A West Coast butterfly. The upperside is basically blackish brown, crossed by bands of large creamy spots. Setting it apart from the other banded admirals are its orange forewing tips. Males establish and defend territories, often on willow branches. This one visits spreading dogbane, a favorite source of nectar for many butterflies. (119)

White Admiral Southern Canada and the northeastern United States are home to the White Admiral, also known as the Banded Purple. It is not very purple, but its black is rich and deep. Beyond the milk-white bands lie rows of bright blue crescents, the innermost of these on the hindwings being capped with russet. Birches are the preferred hosts. (120)

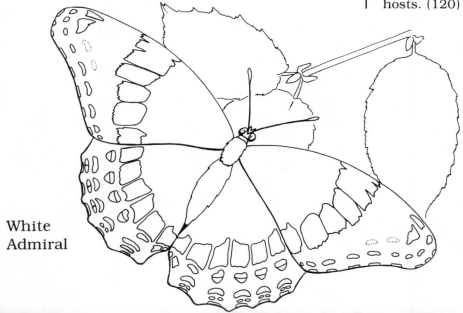

White
Admiral

California Sister The name comes from the butterfly's colors, black with white bands. They reminded someone of a nun's habit. However, the wings also have a bright orange patch on the tip of the forewing. Rusty orange bars highlight the wings, especially beneath, and the underside has purplish blue bands along the border and body. Sisters avidly visit rotting plums and other fruits. (121)

Red-spotted Purple Sometimes regarded as the same species as Banded Purples, minus the bands. The upperside, shown on this basking Purple, is shiny blue-black, with blue concentrated toward the edges of the hindwings. In the Southeastern Woods Scene (p. 41) you will see the underside. Color it blackish brown with brick-red spots, blue-barred along the margins. (122)

Pavon The pattern of Pavon suggests the admirals, but it is actually related to the hackberry butterflies. Dusky whitish bands cross the wings, which shine deep purple when struck by direct sunshine. The patches near the forewing tips glow bright orange. Very different, the underside is light tan with a white band, black eyespots, and brown lines. Pavon lives mostly in Mexico, but drifts into Texas occasionally. (123)

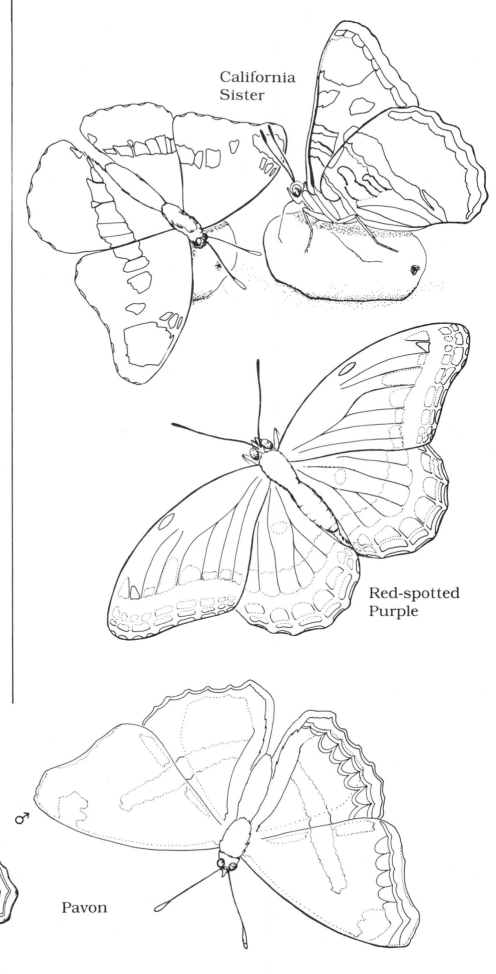

California Sister

Red-spotted Purple

♂

Pavon

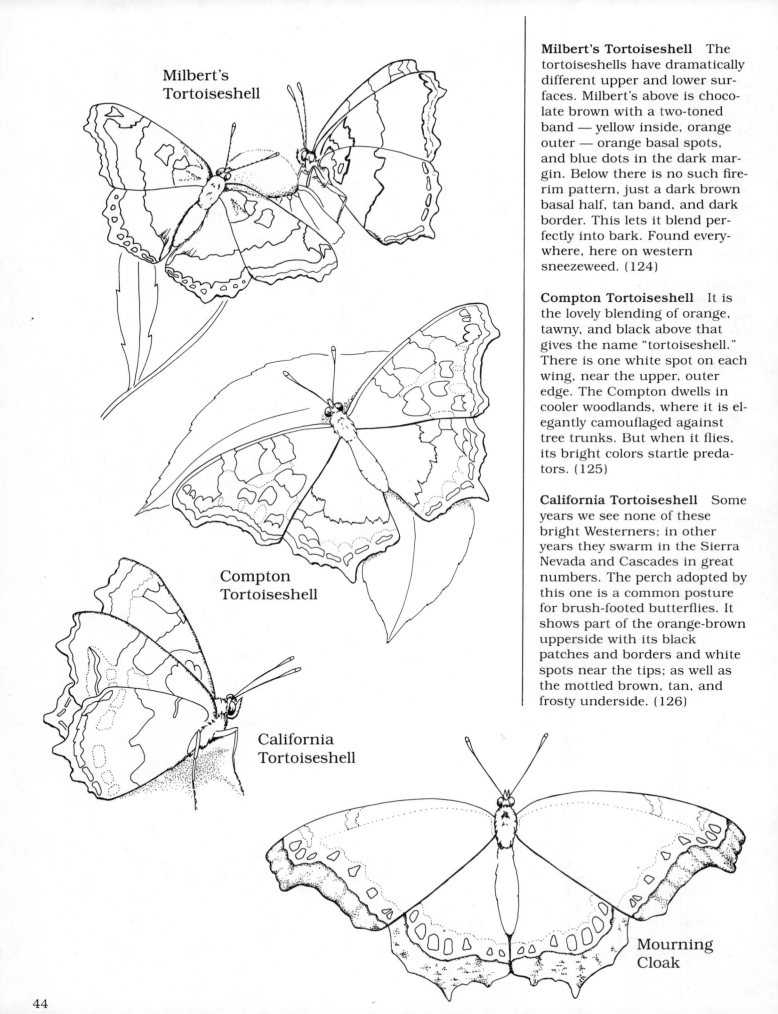

Milbert's
Tortoiseshell

Compton
Tortoiseshell

California
Tortoiseshell

Mourning
Cloak

Milbert's Tortoiseshell The tortoiseshells have dramatically different upper and lower surfaces. Milbert's above is chocolate brown with a two-toned band — yellow inside, orange outer — orange basal spots, and blue dots in the dark margin. Below there is no such fire-rim pattern, just a dark brown basal half, tan band, and dark border. This lets it blend perfectly into bark. Found everywhere, here on western sneezeweed. (124)

Compton Tortoiseshell It is the lovely blending of orange, tawny, and black above that gives the name "tortoiseshell." There is one white spot on each wing, near the upper, outer edge. The Compton dwells in cooler woodlands, where it is elegantly camouflaged against tree trunks. But when it flies, its bright colors startle predators. (125)

California Tortoiseshell Some years we see none of these bright Westerners; in other years they swarm in the Sierra Nevada and Cascades in great numbers. The perch adopted by this one is a common posture for brush-footed butterflies. It shows part of the orange-brown upperside with its black patches and borders and white spots near the tips; as well as the mottled brown, tan, and frosty underside. (126)

44

Question Mark This eastern anglewing has two seasonal forms. The summer form's hindwings are almost completely black. On the fall form, both the fore- and hindwings are bright reddish orange with heavy brown markings. Both forms have a lilac-purple border, narrower on the black-spotted summer butterflies. The autumn generation lives through the winter as adults, in turn producing the summer form generation. (127)

Satyr Anglewing In common with the tortoiseshells, anglewings possess ragged wing margins that help their dull undersides blend in with leaves and bark. The Satyr, a western butterfly, is the brightest of all anglewings — fiery light orange turning to golden toward the tails of the hindwings, marked with inky spots and reddish brown borders. The spiny caterpillars eat stinging nettle. (128)

Gray Comma Commas and Question Marks are anglewings. Their names refer to tiny silver marks on the underside of the hindwing. Otherwise, the underside is grayish brown with darker striations and a frosty forewing tip. The upperside is reddish tawny, brown spotted and bordered, with orange dots in the broad hindwing border. Commas are fleet, but often return to one spot. (129)

Mourning Cloak (p. 44) Nothing else looks like a Mourning Cloak, well known by sight if not by name. The body and the larger part of the wings are deep chocolate brown with maroon reflections. Long rows of deep blue spots run all around the wings just inside the light yellow borders. Actually a tortoiseshell, the Mourning Cloak flies all over and likes elms and willows. (130)

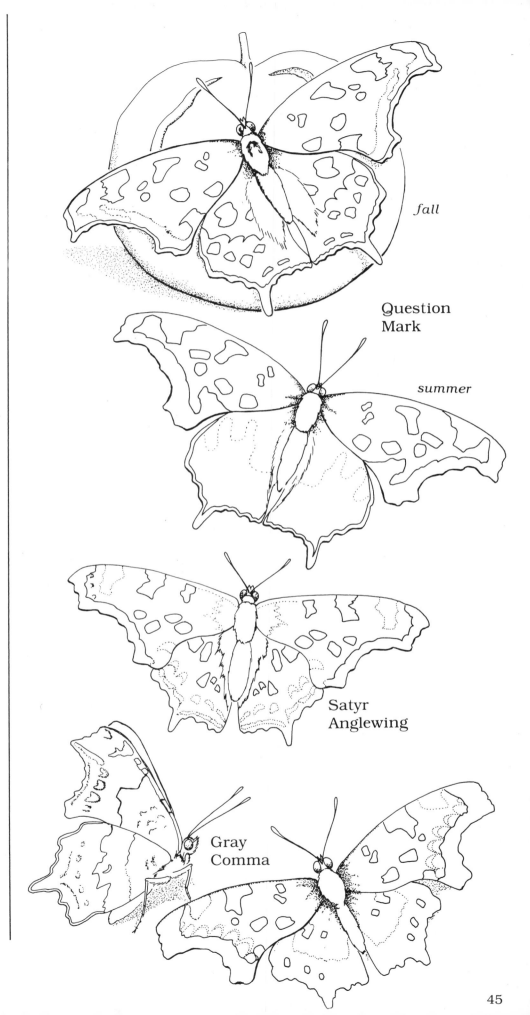

fall

Question Mark

summer

Satyr Anglewing

Gray Comma

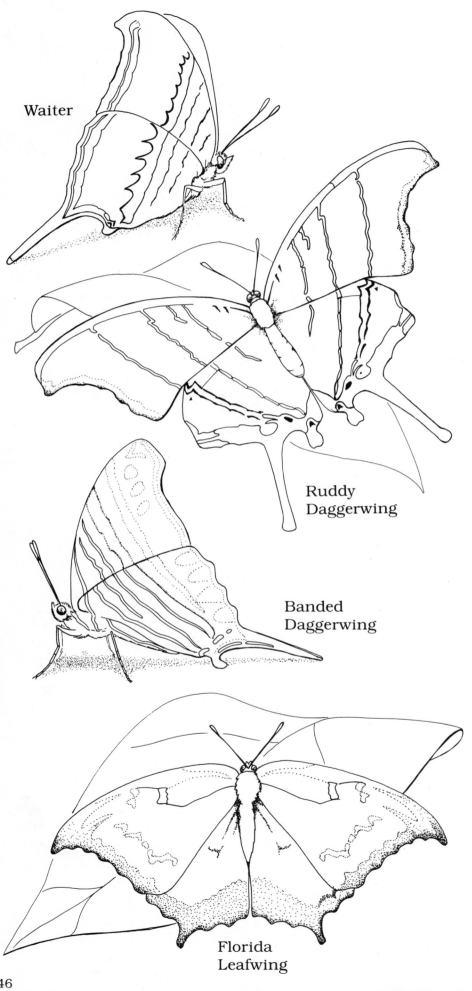

Waiter

Ruddy
Daggerwing

Banded
Daggerwing

Florida
Leafwing

Waiter This common tropical butterfly turns up occasionally in southern Texas. The upperside is dark brown. Beneath, as seen here, the crisp white inner half of the wings contrasts with the brown outer part. A reddish streak lines the white part, another runs around the outer edge to the shorter of the tails, ending in a blue spot. The pattern suggests a waiter's uniform. (131)

Ruddy Daggerwing The strange-shaped wings end in "dagger" tails. They are colored ruddy orange, with dark brown stripes and tails. A resident of southern Florida. The caterpillar feeds on fig leaves and the adult on the fig fruit. In spite of the very different names and colors, the shapes tell you that the Ruddy Daggerwing and the Waiter are close relatives. (132)

Banded Daggerwing Another tropical brush-foot, this species lives as far north as Texas and Florida. The outer half of the underside is reddish tan, with two violet bands running across. The inner half has rusty lines across a silky white background. The body, too, is white. (133)

Florida Leafwing Woodlands in southern Florida where croton grows may host this brilliant butterfly. The upperside, flaming red-orange, is startling when it flashes nearby. Then, when the leafwing alights, the bright color disappears from sight; the underside is colored like a dead leaf, and the wing shape enhances the camouflage. (134)

Goatweed Butterfly The name of this common southeastern leafwing comes from its caterpillar's host plant, Goatweed (also known as croton). This female is tawny orange above with brown along the edges and invading the wings. Rainy season individuals have longer tails (colored violet) and more pointed wingtips than those of drier months. Goatweed Butterflies are very speedy fliers, but they will come to a bait of rotting fruit. (135)

Buckeye The big eyespots that give it its name have yellow rims and black, blue, and violet centers. Most of the rest of the upperside is warm brown, but there are two orange bars on each forewing, a buff band outside them, and orange below the hindwing eyespots. Among the many flowers visited by this fast flier is plantain, also one of its host plants. Great Buckeye migrations take place in the fall. (136)

Hackberry Butterfly Confined to the leaves of hackberry trees for food, this butterfly's caterpillars are jade green. Both they and the green chrysalids blend beautifully with the foliage. When this butterfly closes its wings you see a complicated pattern of brown lines on a purplish white background and rows of black, white-centered, yellow-rimmed eyespots. (137)

Tawny Emperor Another hackberry feeder, more common in the Southeast than elsewhere. Its forewings are colored rich reddish tawny, with black bars and bands and rows of golden spots. The hindwings, tawny at the base, become black outwardly with rows of tawny-ringed black spots. Here it is visiting rotting orange persimmons, a favorite. (138)

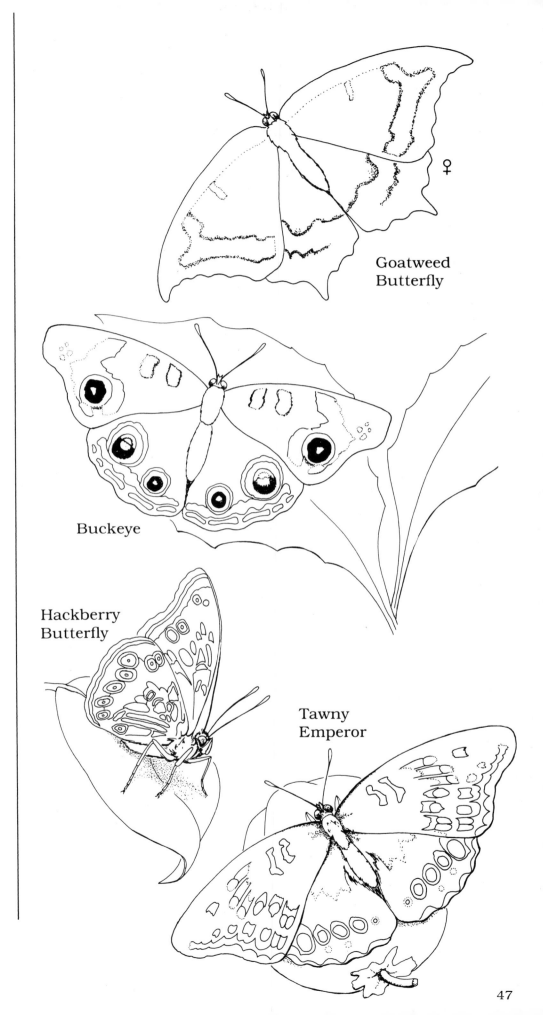

♀

Goatweed
Butterfly

Buckeye

Hackberry
Butterfly

Tawny
Emperor

47

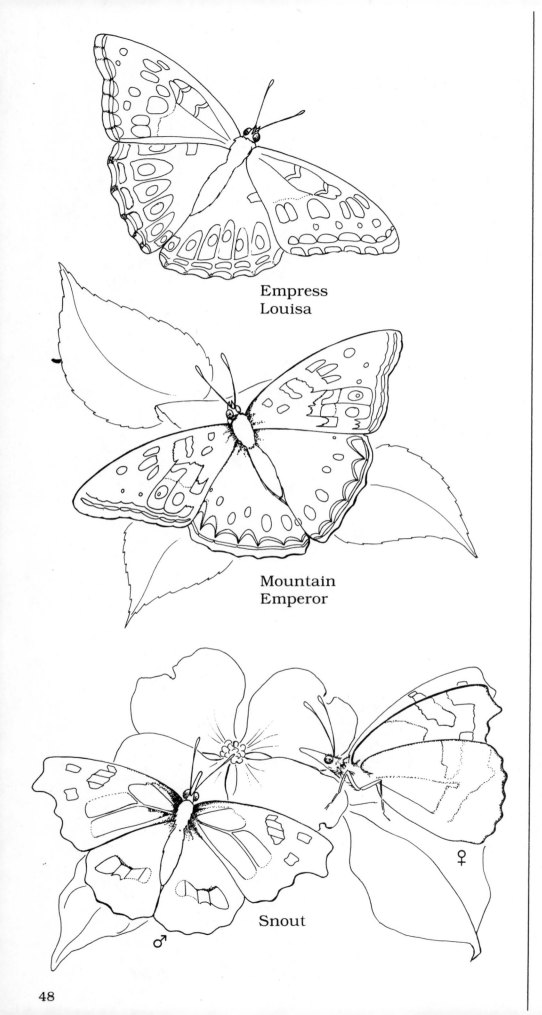

Empress
Louisa

Mountain
Emperor

Snout

♀

♂

Empress Louisa   This is a fairly recently discovered hackberry butterfly of south Texas and Mexico. Her wings, a warm, light brown, are blackish around the tips, where there are white spots. The unpupilled black eyespots around the hindwings have tan rims, and the hindwing scalloping is dark brown. (139)

Mountain Emperor   Reigns in southwestern canyons where hackberry trees grow wild. The Mountain Emperor has the usual hackberry butterfly pattern, lighter toward the body and darker outward, with white spots and black eyelike circles. Its color, however, is a richer, redder brown than that of most of its relatives. (140)

Snout Butterfly   Like the previous four species, although not at all closely related, the Snout feeds on hackberries. It is remarkable for the long "snout" formed by its palpi sticking straight out in front of its face. Its great migrations are also notable. The upperside is dark brown with creamy spots toward the clipped wingtip and large tawny patches on each wing. Beneath, the hindwing and forewing tip are mottled with mauve and cocoa; the forewing base is orange. Nectaring here on Florida dogwood. (141)

Desert Scene

The southwestern desert is arid but far from barren. It comes alive after the spring rains, brimming with wildflowers and butterflies. A male Dogface (33) flaps through the desert on powerful wings. The Pima Orangetip (37), bright yellow and orange, drinks at a western wallflower of the same colors. Mauve Mojave aster hosts a thirsty Bordered Patch (101). A Red-bordered Brown (176), straying from nearby pinewoods, rests in the grass. Searching for yuccas on which to lay her eggs, a speedy Yucca Giant Skipper (191) shoots through.

Desert Scene

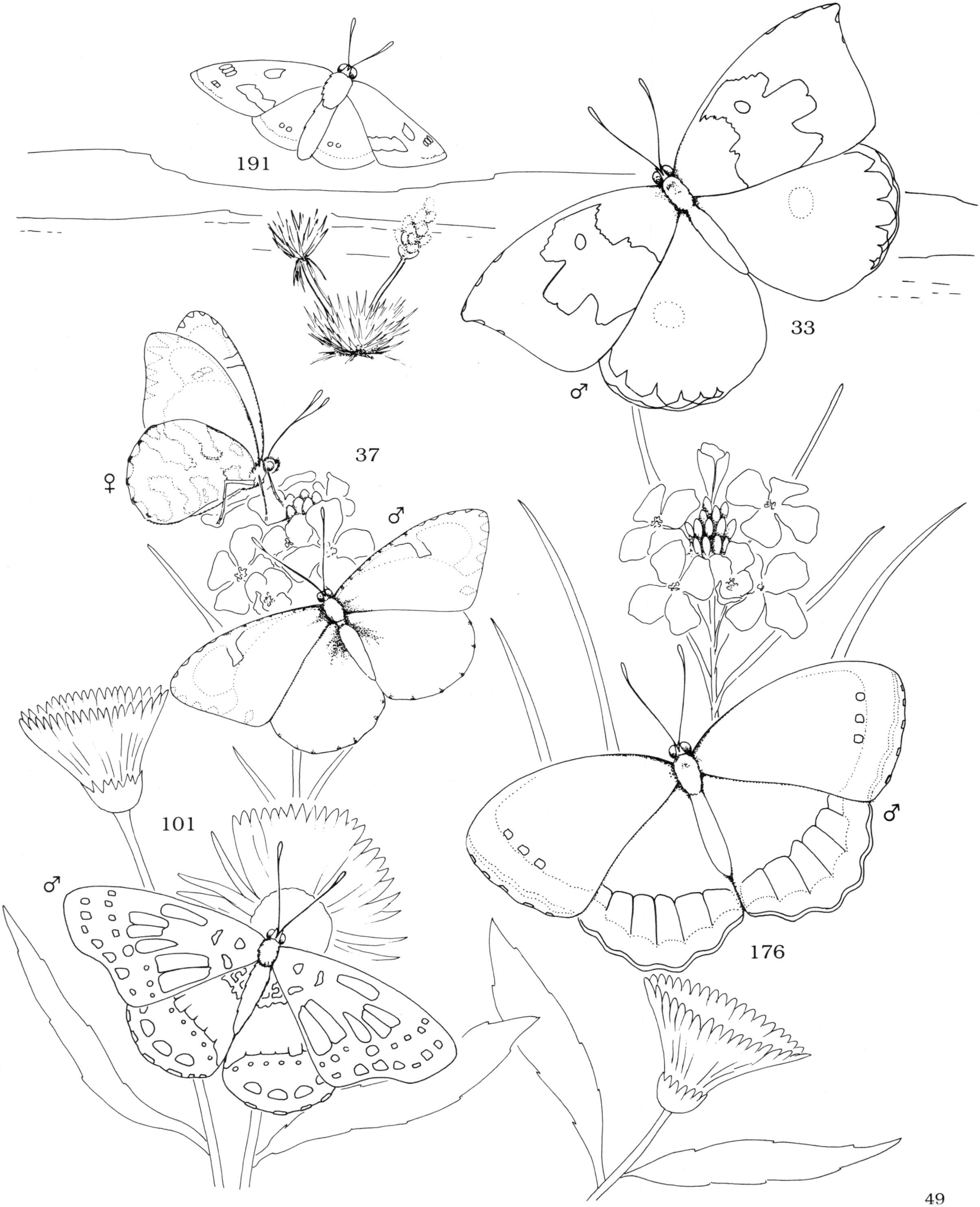

191

33

♂

37

♀

♂

101

♂

♂

176

49

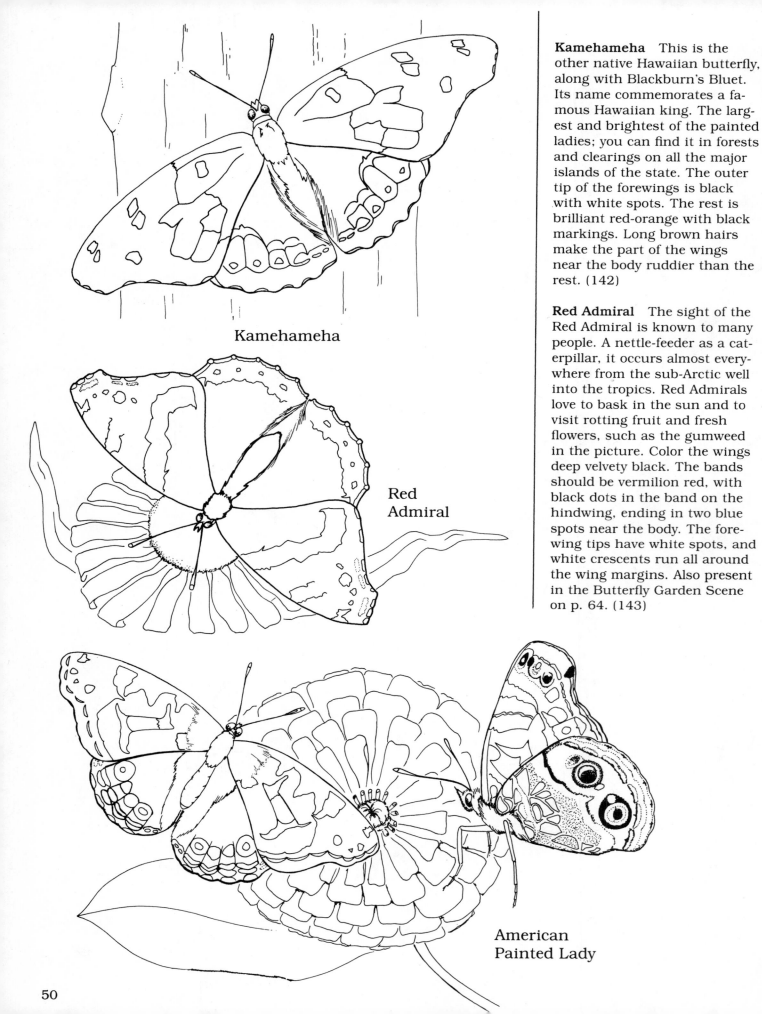

Kamehameha This is the other native Hawaiian butterfly, along with Blackburn's Bluet. Its name commemorates a famous Hawaiian king. The largest and brightest of the painted ladies; you can find it in forests and clearings on all the major islands of the state. The outer tip of the forewings is black with white spots. The rest is brilliant red-orange with black markings. Long brown hairs make the part of the wings near the body ruddier than the rest. (142)

Red Admiral The sight of the Red Admiral is known to many people. A nettle-feeder as a caterpillar, it occurs almost everywhere from the sub-Arctic well into the tropics. Red Admirals love to bask in the sun and to visit rotting fruit and fresh flowers, such as the gumweed in the picture. Color the wings deep velvety black. The bands should be vermilion red, with black dots in the band on the hindwing, ending in two blue spots near the body. The forewing tips have white spots, and white crescents run all around the wing margins. Also present in the Butterfly Garden Scene on p. 64. (143)

Kamehameha

Red
Admiral

American
Painted Lady

West Coast Lady This Pacific Slope butterfly looks much like its close relative, the Painted Lady. The field marks with which to tell it apart (and color it) are these: The bar in a black area at the end of the cell on the upper forewing is orange; the eyespots on the upper hindwing are big and blue; and the brown and white mottling below has a yellowish cast to it. Otherwise the color above is orange-peel orange, with black markings and white spots. The orange shows on the base of the forewing beneath. The butterfly is shown visiting cheeseweed, a host plant. (144)

American Painted Lady (p. 50) Colored like the other ladies except pinker, especially below on the lower half of the forewing. The hindwing blue spots are prominent on the upperside and very large below, where they have black and yellow rings around them. Generally light brown below with white bands and network. Also known as Hunter's Butterfly. More common in the East, and here shown nectaring on red zinnia. (145)

Painted Lady It is not surprising to see this familiar butterfly on a thistle, for that is the larval host plant. Painted Ladies cannot take the northern winter, but they fly north every year from milder regions. Since it can be found all over the world, the Painted Lady's other name is Cosmopolitan Butterfly. Salmon orange is the main color, pinker on the underside of the basal forewing. White spots stand out on the black tips, and blue spots run around the hindwing. Mottled brown and white on the underside. (146)

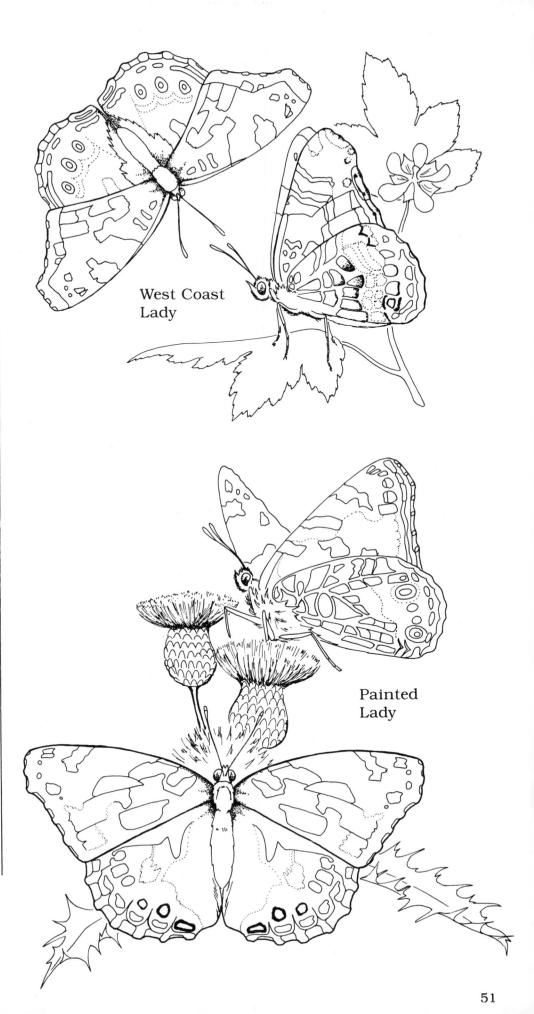

West Coast
Lady

Painted
Lady

51

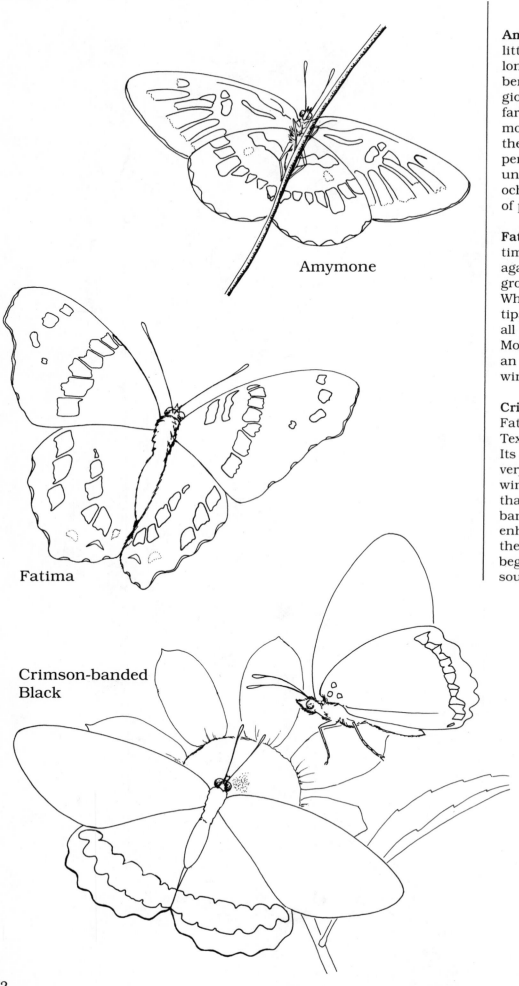

Amymone

Fatima

Crimson-banded
Black

Amymone This frail-looking little butterfly sometimes flies long distances in great numbers. Its usual home is the region of the Gulf of Mexico and farther south. The upperside is mostly gray, but here we see the underside, as it normally perches with wings closed. The underside is mostly a pretty ochre-orange, crossed by bands of pearly white. (147)

Fatima In southern Texas, Fatima flies in early spring and again in late autumn. The ground color is blackish brown. White spots lie in the forewing tips. Vanilla bands sweep cross all wings, ending in red spots. More crimson spots make up an inner band on the hindwings. (148)

Crimson-banded Black Like Fatima, to be found in south Texas — but much more rare. Its simple, striking pattern is very beautiful. The velvety black wings have no markings other than the wavy, bright crimson band, and thin white crescents enhancing the scalloped edge of the hindwings. Nectaring on beggar's tick, a favorite of southern butterflies. (149)

Mimic Here is a very unusual, exotic butterfly supposed to have come to the West Indies with the slave trade. It is found in much of the Old World. The female, pictured above, mimics the African Milkweed Butterfly, a relative of the Monarch. Her wings are bright orange rimmed with black. There are white patches in the black tips and white dots around the black margin. Sometimes called the Blue Moon because of the male's white orbs surrounded by iridescent blue, all set against a night-black background. They are nectaring on lantana. (150)

Florida Purplewing When the direct sunbeams strike a purplewing with its wings open, like this one sucking fruit juice, the wings shimmer with an ultraviolet iridescence. In the shade they look brown, the color of the outer, white-spotted parts in all lights. Spot it in Everglades woodlands. (151)

White Peacock Another butterfly of the Deep South and American tropics, it occasionally wanders north. Wary, it normally perches with its wings closed. The background is pearly white. Pinkish-brown bands and orange lines and crescents mark the wings. Two blue-centered, orange-rimmed eyespots lie in a brown band. The outer margin is salmon orange. (152)

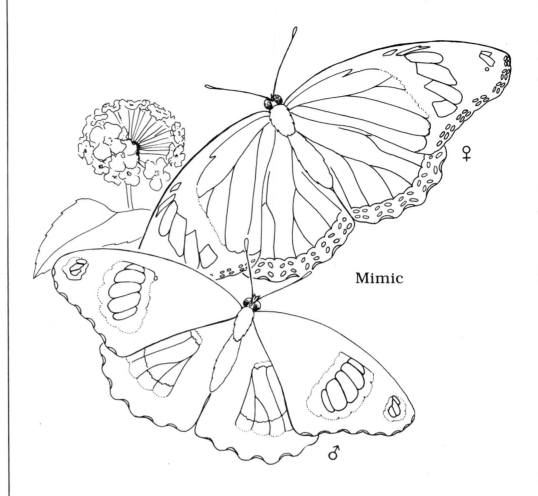

Mimic

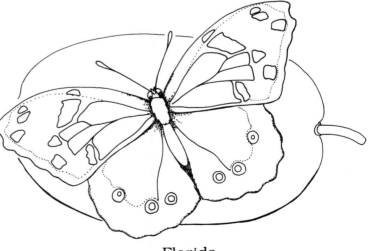

Florida
Purplewing

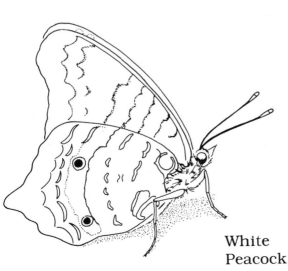

White
Peacock

Prairie Scene

28

104 ♂

86 ♀

♂

163

♀

186

♂

54

Blue Wing The indigo bands of the wings, alternating with black, are deeper than the pale blue of the water hyacinth on which it perches. White spots tip the forewings. Although other kinds of blue wings occur farther south, this one barely makes it to Texas. (153)

Malachite Named for the mineral, which has a lacy green pattern similar to that on the butterfly's wings. They are colored pale jade, interworked with the dark brown that forms the border. Malachites visit Florida from the West Indies, and occur in Texas too. This one visits a spiderwort. (154)

Eighty-eight Butterfly Still another tropical insect that has turned up in Florida rarely. Of course its name comes from the black "88" pattern on the white underside. The base of the underside forewing is pinkish red, the tip black-banded white. The black upperside has light green bands on each wing. (155)

Prairie Scene (p. 54)

When the pioneers arrived they found vast expanses of prairieland. Little remains untouched by the cow and the plow. Where native prairie plants survive in nature reserves, special grassland butterflies may be found. The Regal Fritillary (104) and Dakota Skipper (186) are two of these, both visiting purple coneflower. Commoner butterflies of the plains include the lovely Olympia Marblewing (28), flying through in search of mustard plants; the Prairie Ringlet (163) in the grass; and the Silvery Blue (86) on the coneflower.

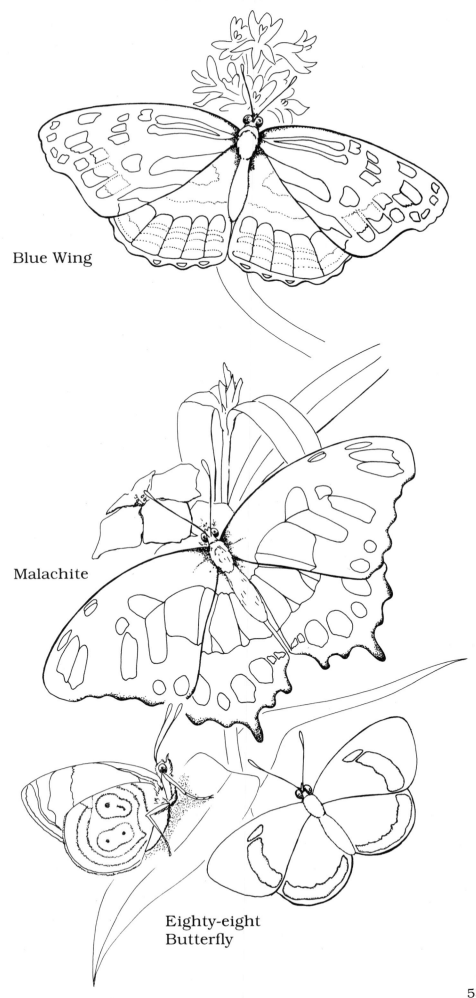

Blue Wing

Malachite

Eighty-eight
Butterfly

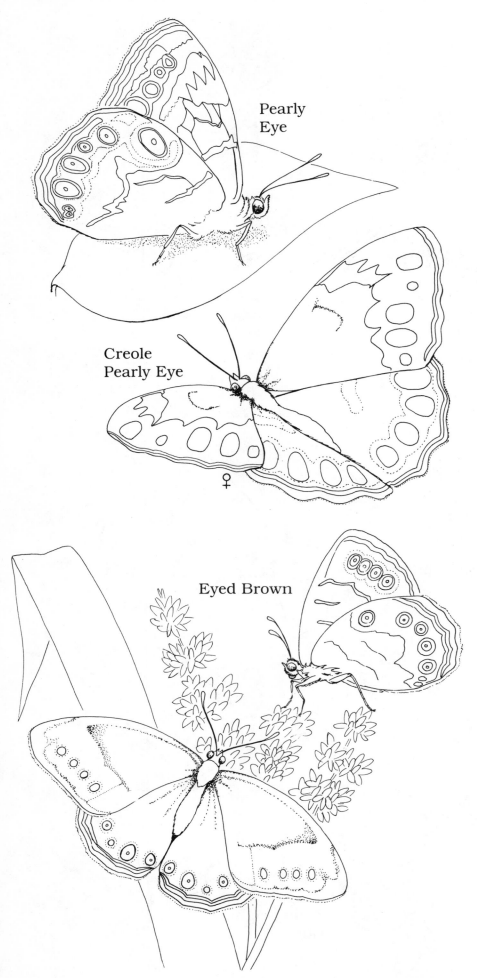

Pearly
Eye

Creole
Pearly Eye

♀

Eyed Brown

Satyrs, Browns, and Wood Nymphs

The family Satyridae may be a subgroup of the brush-footed butterflies. Most of them are colored softly with browns and grays and rusts, and most bear eyespots on their wings. These false eyes serve as targets for birds. Aiming for the "eyes," they miss the butterfly's body. Satyrs haunt woodland glades and meadows where their caterpillars feed on grasses. Almost everywhere grasses grow, some browns fly, including the high arctic.

Pearly Eye This eastern woods-dweller perches on tree trunks and flies rapidly among the dappled shadows. The overall color underneath is light brown, with a lilac hue and a pearly sheen. Brown lines cross the wings, and an orangey line runs around the rims. Lying in a loose buff band, the brown eyespots have orange rings around them and blue or pearly pupils. Also to be found in the Southeastern Woods Scene on p. 41. (156)

Creole Pearly Eye This female seldom shows her upperside except in flight. It is a light buckskin brown, with a pale tan area toward the edge. A long row of black-brown spots runs through this lighter field. She will lay her eggs on maiden cane, after the male locates her within the cane brake. (157)

Eyed Brown Perching on a sedge head, this pair of Eyed Browns are typical satyrs. They disport in moist meadows of the Northeast and Midwest. The upperside presents a warm cocoa-brown aspect with lighter tan patches and blue-black, white-centered, yellow-rimmed eyespots. The pattern repeats below but the color is darker brown with still darker lines and more distinct eyespots. (158)

Large Wood Nymph Also known as the Blue-eyed Grayling, its eyespots are indeed blue and white, centered within black and yellow rings. The butterfly flies over much of the continent and exhibits many forms. The one shown here has the forewing eyespots embedded in a large patch of canary yellow. The rest is light brown striated with dark brown, the outer half of the hindwing paler. Watch for it in woods at their grassy edges, at sap or fruit or nectaring on such flowers as alfalfa. (159)

Great Basin Wood Nymph Visiting yellow sweet clover, this western wood nymph is dark brown with a lighter fringe and pale yellow rings around its black eyespots. The eyespots target bird attacks away from the body of the butterfly. Sagebrush desert and dry, open woods are its favored habitats. (160)

Ochre Ringlet Ochre is the main color of this brightest ringlet — a rich, reddish-gold. The upperside is all ochre, as is most of the forewing below; its tip beyond the yellow-ringed black eyespot is grayish. Color the hindwing olive-gray, except for the buffy lightning-streak across it. Very abundant in the Rocky Mountain states. (161)

Northwest Ringlet Equally common in the grasslands of the Pacific Northwest. It is colored like the Ochre Ringlet, except the ochre is paler and the olive grayer. Usually it lacks the small eyespots. (162)

Prairie Ringlet A third ringlet closely related to the two above. The forewing has an orange streak inward from the eyespot, and the hindwing is quite olive. Like other satyrs, its caterpillars feed on grasses. It appears in the Prairie Scene (p. 54). (163)

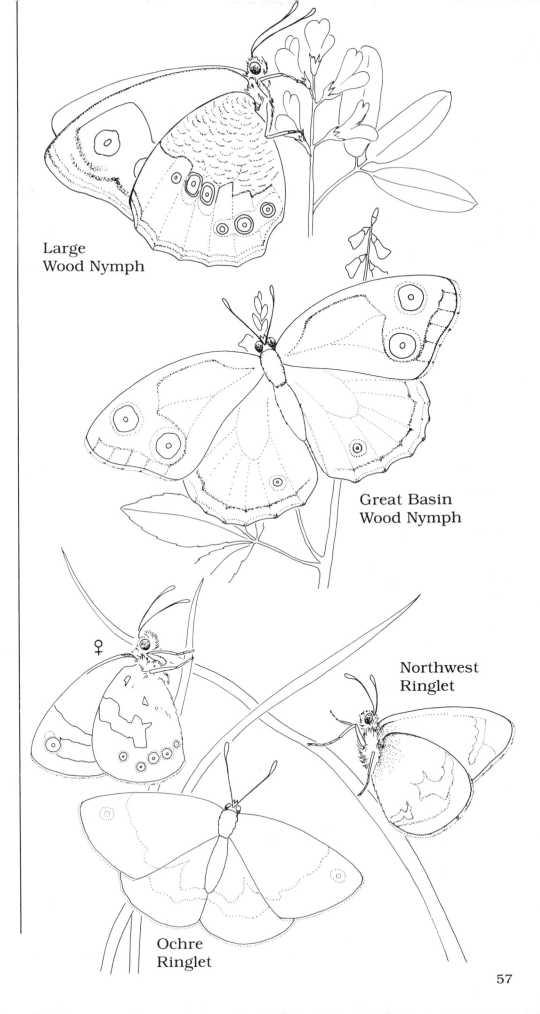

Large Wood Nymph

Great Basin Wood Nymph

Northwest Ringlet

Ochre Ringlet

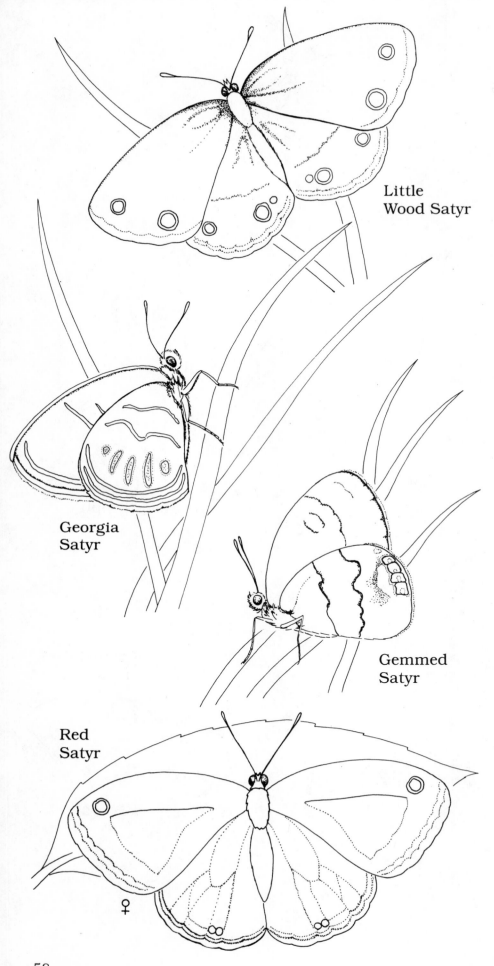

Little
Wood Satyr

Georgia
Satyr

Gemmed
Satyr

Red
Satyr

♀

Little Wood Satyr Like a small wood nymph, the Little Wood Satyr dodges and darts through tall grass with speed and skill. It is the commonest, most widespread of the wood (or grass) satyrs. It is warm brown overall with yellow-ringed, blue-black eyespots inside darker brown lines that edge the wings. (164)

Georgia Satyr This pretty little satyr's hallmarks are long oval eyespots with yellow rims and blue-dotted centers, each situated within an ellipse of brick-red lines. More red lines run along the edge and the base of the wings. This is a southeastern grass satyr. (165)

Gemmed Satyr Its "gems" are blue-and-silver eyespots, gold-rimmed and run together, all set in a metallic silver patch on the hindwing. Faint reddish lines run around the silver patch and across the reddish tan wings. The Gemmed Satyr flies in grassy woods from the Midwest south. (166)

Red Satyr Oak country of the arid Southwest is the place to search for the brightest satyr. The wings on the upperside are broadly copper-red with thick brown outlines. Each wing bears one eyespot, black with yellow rim and pale bluish center. (167)

Mitchell's Marsh Satyr Most of the bogs and marshy meadows required by this butterfly have been drained or developed, placing it at risk. Only in a few spots south of the Great Lakes does it survive. It is colored like the Georgia Satyr except that its eyespots are rounder and more numerous. See it in the Eastern Swamp Scene (p. 13). (168)

White-veined Arctic The arctics are a group of satyrs prevalent in the Far North and in high mountains. They blend well with their backgrounds of rock, lichen, and grass. This one even lives in Labrador and on Greenland. Its forewing is olive-tan, the tip frosty gray like the hindwing with brown speckles. A darker brown band crosses the hindwing, and the veins stand out crisply white. The female's upperside is dull gray-brown, lighter tan on the outer hindwing. (169)

Chryxus Arctic Flies from the arctic-alpine peaks all the way down to sagelands along the Rockies. The female, with her wings spread here, is bright tawny, paler toward the olive-brown margins. Her eyespots are black with tiny white pupils. (170)

Arctic Grayling Haunts the arctic tundra from Sweden to Siberia to Hudson Bay. The forewing is reddish tawny with a frosty tip. The frostiness covers much of the hindwing, which has a tan band near the outer edge and a brown one across the middle. (171)

Magdalena Alpine The only all-black, unmarked butterfly in America, weathering to a soft brown plush. Magdalena lives only on high mountain rockslides, where males fly up and down in search of females. They pause to sip nectar from pink moss campion, which is where you will find Magdalena, in the Alpine Scene on p. 20. (172)

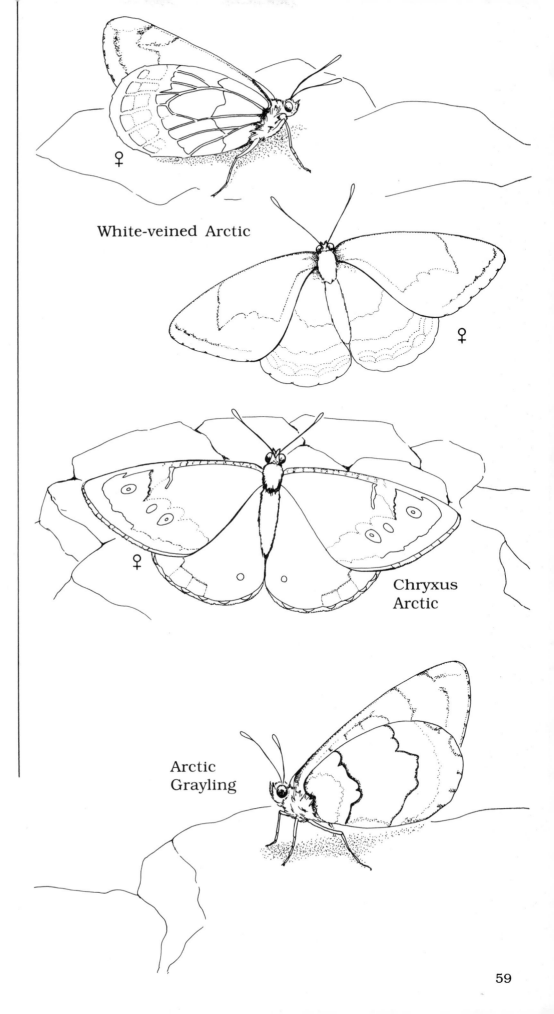

White-veined Arctic

Chryxus Arctic

Arctic Grayling

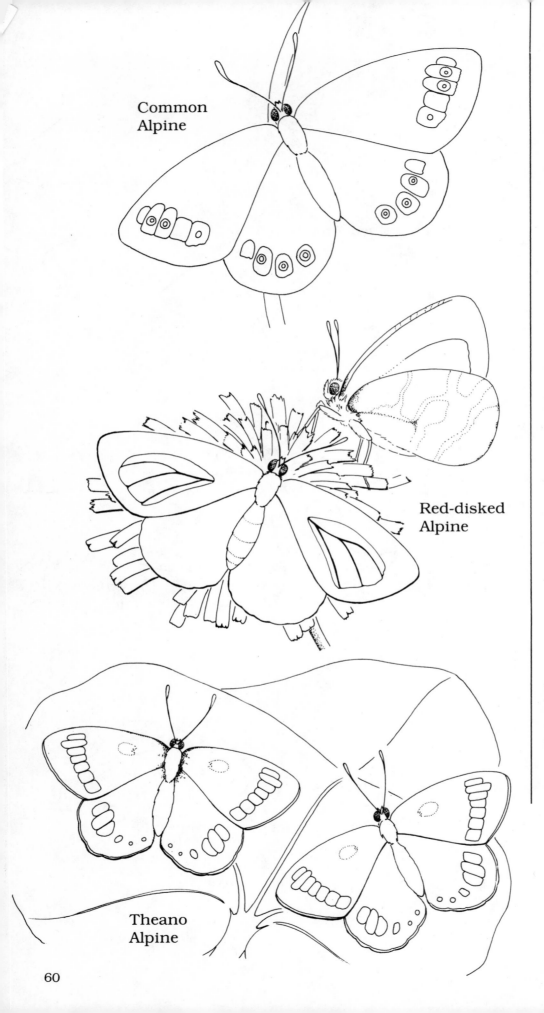

Common
Alpine

Red-disked
Alpine

Theano
Alpine

Common Alpine Also called Butler's Alpine. It has a pattern typical of many alpines of the European Alps: chocolate brown wings ringed by black, white-centered eyespots lying in cinnamon patches. A fresh alpine shimmers with a purplish green iridescence. Lives in western mountain meadows and clearings. (173)

Red-disked Alpine Repeating the common alpine color scheme of deep brown and rusty-red, this species lacks the eyespots of most other alpines. The rusty disk shows below, but the brown is clouded with frosty gray scaling, especially the outer portions of the wings. Asian and Alaskan, it also flies all across Canada and southward in the Great Lakes states. Here it nectars on a dandelion, a favorite of many butterflies. (174)

Theano Alpine Two Theano Alpines confront one another on leaves of marsh marigold, a perching site much favored by these smallest of our alpines. Their high-country colonies tend to be tight but well populated. Russet rings of spots surround the dark brown wings. Beneath, the hindwing spots are yellow. (175)

Red-bordered Brown A big satyr, mostly Mexican in range, it is shown in the Desert Scene (p. 49). Piney aridlands are its home, on desert edges. There it flies in late summer and autumn. The scalloped, velvety brown wings run to cocoa on the outer forewing, cinnamon-red on the hindwing border. (176)

Skippers

Skippers resemble moths in some ways, with thick, hairy bodies and short wings. Most are small and speedy, with a skipping flight. Skippers that are triangular and tawny tend to be grass feeders, while the others use many host plants. Skippers succeed in many sorts of habitats and love flowers and mud. Their family is the Hesperiidae. The fast flying Giant Skippers (see example, p. 65) have their own family, the Megathymidae.

Zabulon Skipper   Common in the East. This female visits blue violet for nectar. Her wings are rusty red, heavily speckled with violet on the outer half. Fringe and body are also reddish. (177)

Yehl Skipper   This southeastern skipper flashes by in a golden blur. Perched, it looks very orange, with pale yellow spots and orange legs. Its gold-tipped antennae are short and hooked, as on most skippers. (178)

Sandhill Skipper   The way this skipper is perching, with the hindwings in one plane and the forewings in another, is typical of many skippers. Both the fore- and hindwings are tawny orange with dark edges, and black dashes cross the forewings. (179)

Least Skipperling   Here is one of our tiniest butterflies. Its forewing is bright orange; hindwing, yellow-gold with light veins. The orange repeats on the upper abdomen; otherwise the body is white, eyes black. (180)

Whirlabout   Another golden tawny skipper, brown about the edges, but orange fringed. The black dash on the forewing is called a skipper's stigma. The name reflects its speedy, orbiting flight habits. Appears in Southeastern Woods Scene (p. 41). (181)

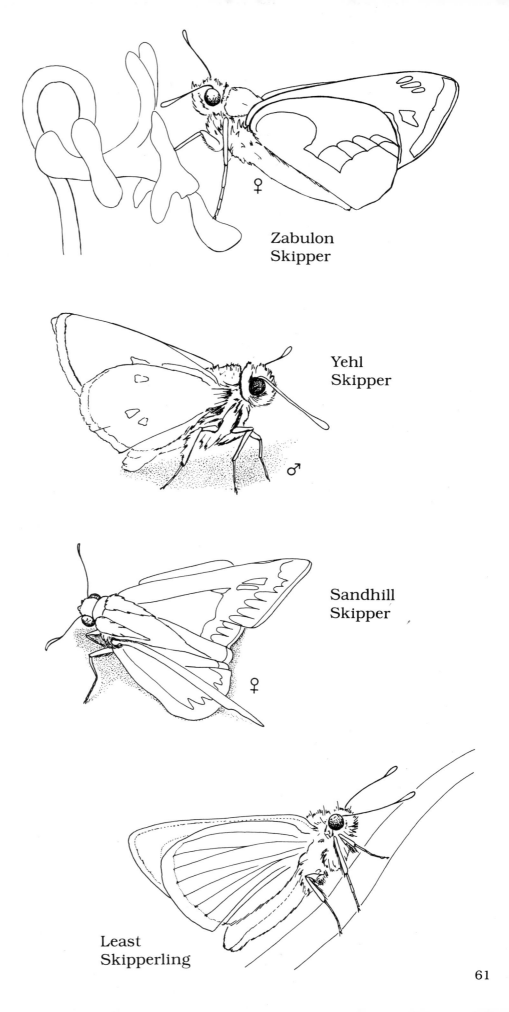

Zabulon
Skipper

Yehl
Skipper

Sandhill
Skipper

Least
Skipperling

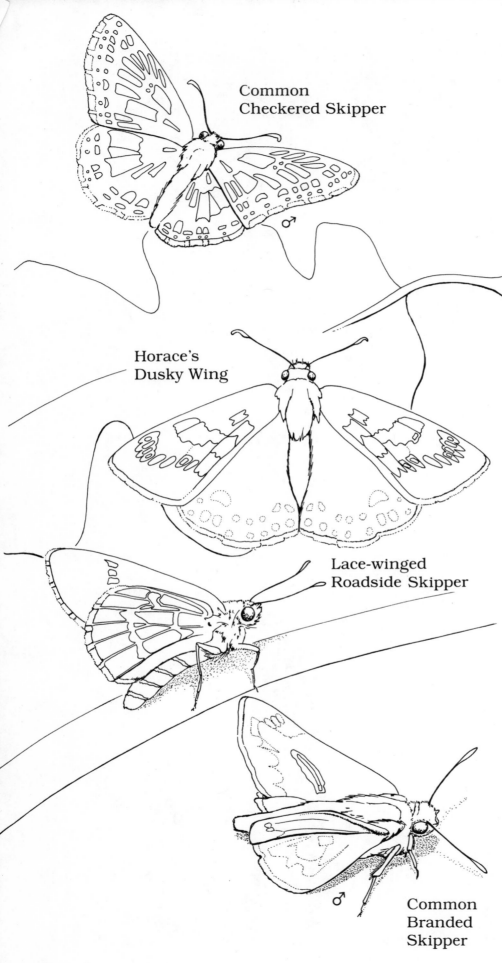

Common
Checkered Skipper

♂

Horace's
Dusky Wing

Lace-winged
Roadside Skipper

♂

Common
Branded
Skipper

Common Checkered Skipper
A very common sight in fields and vacant lots. Charcoal wings checked with white. Fringe white, black checked. Bluish furry scales on the body reflect iridescently. (182)

Horace's Duskywing The colors of the wings are soft but complex in pattern. Generally chestnut brown, with pale spots around the hindwings, black patches and glossy white dots on the forewings. An oak feeder. (183)

Lace-winged Roadside Skipper
The many species of roadside skippers look rather alike. This one is distinctive for the lacy pattern of creamy markings intersected by white veins against olive-gray wings. (184)

Common Branded Skipper
The wings above are tawny basally, brown marginally, with a black stigma on the forewing and light fringes. The gold pattern on the upperside is repeated in bright silvery marks underneath. Found in many forms and many habitats across the Northern Hemisphere, always among grasses. (185)

Dakota Skipper Since this uncommon skipper is so closely linked to native prairie grasslands, you will find it in the Prairie Scene on p. 54. Made rare by the plowing and grazing of the prairies, the Dakota Skipper survives in a number of nature reserves, where it loves to visit purple coneflower. The caterpillars eat native grasses. (186)

Guava Skipper The larvae of this robust Latin American skipper feed on guava leaves, while the adults like the fruits. It is superbly colored: Matte-black wings highlighted by white fringes, two scarlet spots on the forewing edge, and shiny blue-green streaks and reflections. The red repeats on its head, the blue on the skipper's body. (187)

Silver-spotted Skipper A big, fast flier, it is common in parks and gardens. Here it visits Japanese honeysuckle, showing the large silver patch on the underside of the hindwing, the gold one on the forewing. Otherwise the wings are a bright brown. (188)

Long-tailed Skipper Luckily, this spectacular skipper is very common in the South. So prevalent, in fact, that it holds vast migrations. The wings are brown, the spots and head are golden. Tails gold-rimmed. Long furry scales clothe the body, rendering it and the bases of the wings iridescent turquoise in the sunshine. It is nectaring on pickerelweed. (189)

Flashing Astraptes This tropic beauty also has a turquoise body, but its head is blue-green, too. The bases of the wings shimmer metallic sky-blue, and the outer forewing bars are opalescent, white but reflecting green. All this against basic black. (190)

Yucca Giant Skipper Different species of giant skippers live throughout the Southwest, all of them feeding on yucca or agave as larvae. The caterpillars burrow into the roots of those spiny plants. Giant Skippers fly at great speed, this one across the Desert Scene (p. 49). It is blackish brown with yellow patches and a white bar. (191)

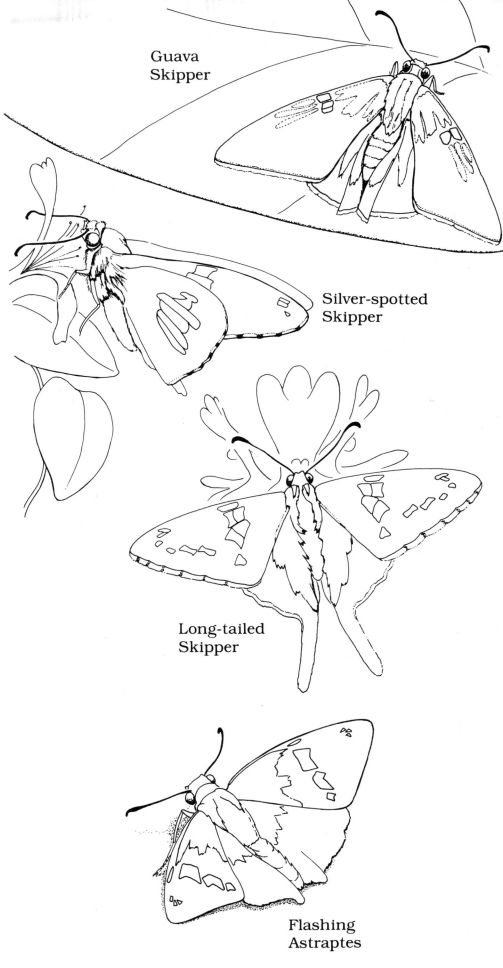

Guava
Skipper

Silver-spotted
Skipper

Long-tailed
Skipper

Flashing
Astraptes

Butterfly Garden Scene

Any gardener can attract butterflies into the yard by gardening with host plants and nectar-bearing flowers. Nettles are needed for the Red Admiral (143). Monarchs (113) will both breed and nectar on butterfly weed, a great attractant for others, too. Three Spring Azures (74) flit over holly. The top two are a courting pair. The Common Sulphur (32), in flight, will breed on white clover in the lawn. The Tiger Swallowtail (3) avidly visits buddleia, or butterfly bush, a great shrub for butterfly gardens.

123

124

125

126

127

127

128

129

130

131

132

133

134

135

♂

♀

136

137

138

139

140

141

♂

♀

142

143

144

145

146

147

148

149

150

♀

♂

151

152

153

154

155

156

157

♀

158

159